The Writing Challenge

HIGH POINT UNIVERSITY
SMITH LIBRARY
UNIVERSITY STATION, MONTLIEU AVE.
HIGH POINT, NC 27262-3598

The Writing Challenge

KAREN BATCHELOR
RANDI SLAUGHTER

HEINLE & HEINLE PUBLISHERS
A Division of Wadsworth, Inc.
Boston, Massachusetts 02116

For giving us inspiration, encouragement, and wonderful examples to follow:

John Dennis

Donna Ilyin

Lois Wilson

Virginia Biagi

LIBRARY OF CONGRESS CATALOGING-IN-PUBLICATION DATA

Batchelor, Karen.
  The writing challenge / Karen Batchelor, Randi Slaughter.
    p. cm.
  ISBN 0-8384-3377-4
  1. English language--Textbooks for foreign speakers. 2. English language--Rhetoric. I. Slaughter, Randi. II. Title.
  PE1128.B37 1990
  428.2'4--dc20   89-13772
                                                           CIP

Copyright © 1991 by Heinle & Heinle Publishers,
a division of Wadsworth, Inc.

All rights reserved. No part of this book may be reproduced or transmitted in any form or by any means, electronic or mechanical, including photocopying, recording, or any information storage and retrieval system, without permission in writing from the Publisher.

This book was set in 11/13 Baskerville by Ruttle, Shaw & Wetherill, Inc., and printed and bound by Viking Press. The cover was printed by Lehigh Press.

Printing: 2 3 4 5 6 7   Year: 3 4 5 6 7

Printed in the U.S.A.

ISBN 0-8384-3377-4

Illustration Credit: Shelley Matheis

Photo Credits: pp. 1 left (Russian family) and right (flamenco dancer, Spain), and 109 right (Indian woman): UPI/Bettmann Newsphotos. pp. 1 bottom; 2; 19 left, right, and bottom; 73 bottom; and 82 top right: Maggie Barbieri. pp. 8, 20, 23, 37 bottom, 38, 43, 61, 74, 82 left and middle, 91 bottom, 98 left and right, and 110 left and right: Eric Liebowitz. p. 26: Eileen Prince. pp. 37 left and right, and 44: Sona Doran. p. 41: Dept. of Labor Statistics. pp. 55 left (celebrating festival, Kalibo, in Philippines) and right (Athenians in carnival costume), and 109 left (traditionally dressed ethnic Hungarian refugees, Budapest): Reuters/Bettmann Newsphotos. p. 62: Steve Dick, The University of Kansas, University Relations Center. pp. 73 left, and 80: Mary Goss. p. 78: The Bettmann Archive. p. 82 bottom right: April Blair Stewart. pp. 91 left and right, and 109 bottom: Karen Peratt.

INTRODUCTION

The fact that most ESL students have a problem with writing is hardly news. That their ability to succeed in other areas often depends on their ability to write is also painfully true. Writing is empowerment, and adult ESL students have a wide range of writing needs: some academic, some vocational, some survival, and some simply personal.

That we should be putting more emphasis on the teaching of writing is not in question. Both the academic and business communities are currently concerned with the improvement of writing skills. However, the debate on *how* to teach writing continues. Traditionalists put the emphasis squarely on the product (for example, "Write an essay comparing and contrasting your country to the United States.") and spend endless hours correcting the end result. Proponents of the newer "process approach" tend to assume that the process of writing is much more important than the final product, often overlooking one major reason for writing in the first place—to be able to write an acceptable paper.

The ideal writing curriculum for ESL students should focus on both the process and the product. *The Writing Challenge* does just that. It is the first book at this level to focus on a multitude of process techniques aimed at helping students to generate ideas and plan compositions while still holding students accountable for a wide variety of finished products. These products include both letter and essay format and styles ranging from personal narrative to formal comparison.

The Writing Challenge contains seven units of eight lessons each for a total of fifty-six one-hour lessons. Additionally, the *Teacher's Manual* includes suggestions for review lessons and for lessons using resources outside the classroom. The last lesson of each unit is a quiz.

While the objective of each unit is for students to produce one major piece of polished writing, it is also important for students to write regularly. To achieve both of these goals, each unit is organized in the following manner:

LESSON ONE	Introduction to the topic. Quick paragraph writing.
LESSON TWO	Reading and journal writing.
LESSON THREE	Major editing and paraphrasing exercise.
LESSON FOUR	Ordering and peer-editing exercise.
LESSON FIVE	Writing from picture prompts.
LESSON SIX	First draft of major writing. Vocabulary review.
LESSON SEVEN	Second draft of major writing. Connecting words.
LESSON EIGHT	Unit test.

All lessons contain both discussion and writing components. Additionally, each individual lesson begins with a short vocabulary list and exercise. This vocabulary is designed to familiarize students with common recurring English word patterns (for example, require–requirement; encourage–encouragement). In order for students to internalize these patterns successfully, in this book they have been limited to *-ment*, *-ion*, and *-ness* noun endings, and *-ful*, *-ed*, *-ing*, and *-ous* adjective endings. These patterns are recycled throughout the text.

The Writing Challenge is designed to be used in a 15–18 week semester. It has, however, been used successfully in programs of different lengths. It is a composition book for students in adult, community college, and university settings. It may also be appropriately used in some high-school programs for LEP students as well as in EFL classrooms outside the United States. The book is labeled *intermediate*, although this may cause some confusion because of the disparity of meaning in such labels as *beginning, intermediate,* and *advanced.*

The subject matter in *The Writing Challenge* is not academic. The students are asked to use themselves as their chief resources. However, many of the skills they learn by using this text are those that are useful in an academic setting: taking notes, paraphrasing, writing from notes, editing, building vocabulary, taking tests, and writing narrative essays.

Students using this book should be familiar with the five basic tenses of English: present continuous, simple past, future, simple present, and present perfect.

The Writing Challenge, by focusing on process as well as giving attention to vocabulary development, the use of models, and editing practice, gives students a solid foundation in the fundamentals of writing. Its use of a wide variety of prewriting activities helps students to develop such critical thinking skills as interpreting, organizing, summarizing, imagining, recognizing and recalling data, and comparing/contrasting. The careful combination of these features makes *The Writing Challenge* a unique and practical classroom text.

ACKNOWLEDGMENTS

We thank the following people for reading and classroom testing the manuscript; their comments and suggestions were invaluable: Carole Glanzer, Gordon Howell, Judy Olsen, Leah Oman, Glen Simpson, Keith Surrey, and Matthew Schultz. We also thank our colleague, Dale Silver, for her help in typing the manuscript.

K.B.
R.S.

CONTENTS

INTRODUCTION p. v

UNIT ONE: LOOKING AT ONESELF

Major writing task: personal narrative
Vocabulary: *-ion* noun endings, *-ful* adjective endings

Lesson One	p. 2
Lesson Two	p. 4
Lesson Three	p. 6
Lesson Four	p. 8
Lesson Five	p. 10
Lesson Six	p. 12
Lesson Seven	p. 14
Lesson Eight: Quiz	p. 16

UNIT TWO: TALKING ABOUT EDUCATION

Major writing task: letter of advice
Vocabulary: *-ment* noun endings, *-ed* adjective endings

Lesson Nine	p. 20
Lesson Ten	p. 22
Lesson Eleven	p. 24
Lesson Twelve	p. 26
Lesson Thirteen	p. 28
Lesson Fourteen	p. 30
Lesson Fifteen	p. 32
Lesson Sixteen: Quiz	p. 34

UNIT THREE: THINKING ABOUT JOBS

Major writing task: narrative of explication
Vocabulary: *-ent/-ant* adjective endings,
-ed/-ing adjective endings

Lesson Seventeen	p. 38
Lesson Eighteen	p. 40
Lesson Nineteen	p. 42
Lesson Twenty	p. 44
Lesson Twenty-One	p. 46
Lesson Twenty-Two	p. 48
Lesson Twenty-Three	p. 50
Lesson Twenty-Four: Quiz	p. 52

UNIT FOUR: DESCRIBING SOCIAL CUSTOMS

Major writing task: descriptive narrative (customs)
Vocabulary: *-ion* noun endings, *-ment* noun endings,
  -ed adjective endings, *-ful* adjective endings

Lesson Twenty-Five	p. 56
Lesson Twenty-Six	p. 58
Lesson Twenty-Seven	p. 60
Lesson Twenty-Eight	p. 62
Lesson Twenty-Nine	p. 64
Lesson Thirty	p. 66
Lesson Thirty-One	p. 68
Lesson Thirty-Two: Quiz	p. 70

UNIT FIVE: MAKING TRAVEL PLANS

Major writing task: descriptive narrative (places)
Vocabulary: *-ness* noun endings, *-ous* adjective endings

Lesson Thirty-Three	p. 74
Lesson Thirty-Four	p. 76
Lesson Thirty-Five	p. 78
Lesson Thirty-Six	p. 80
Lesson Thirty-Seven	p. 82
Lesson Thirty-Eight	p. 84
Lesson Thirty-Nine	p. 86
Lesson Forty: Quiz	p. 88

UNIT SIX: COMPARING COUNTRIES

Major writing task: narrative (compare and contrast)
Vocabulary: *-al* adjective endings,
  -ment, -ion, -ness noun endings

Lesson Forty-One	p. 92
Lesson Forty-Two	p. 94
Lesson Forty-Three	p. 96
Lesson Forty-Four	p. 98
Lesson Forty-Five	p. 100
Lesson Forty-Six	p. 102
Lesson Forty-Seven	p. 104
Lesson Forty-Eight: Quiz	p. 106

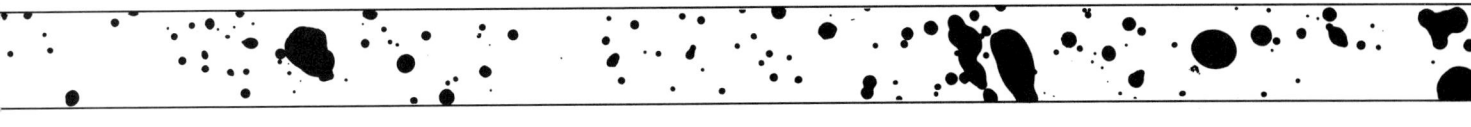

UNIT SEVEN: CONTRASTING CULTURES

Major writing task: narrative (compare and contrast)
Vocabulary: *-al, -ous, -ful, -ed/-ing* adjective endings

Lesson Forty-Nine	p. 110
Lesson Fifty	p. 112
Lesson Fifty-One	p. 114
Lesson Fifty-Two	p. 116
Lesson Fifty-Three	p. 118
Lesson Fifty-Four	p. 120
Lesson Fifty-Five	p. 122
Lesson Fifty-Six: Quiz	p. 124

GLOSSARY   p. 126

EDITING CHECK   p. 131

CONTENT CHECK   p. 133

UNIT I
LOOKING AT ONESELF

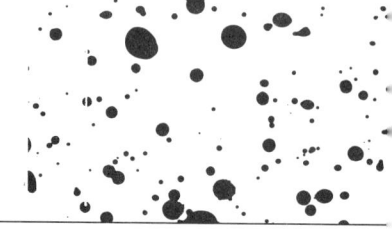

LESSON ONE

VOCABULARY

Verbs **Nouns**

immigrate immigration
describe description

Fill in the blanks with words from the vocabulary list. Be sure the verbs are in the correct tense. The first one is done for you.

1. My family ____*immigrated*____ to the United States two years ago.
2. _____ to the United States can be a problem.
3. I _____ my native country to my friend.
4. Her _____ of her parent's home was interesting.

DISCUSSION ONE

In groups of four or five, take turns introducing yourselves and taking notes. Give your classmates this information.

My name is _____.

I came from _____.

I immigrated here in _____.

I _____
_____.

Listen to the people in your group and take notes about them.

WHO	WHERE FROM	WHEN	COMMENTS

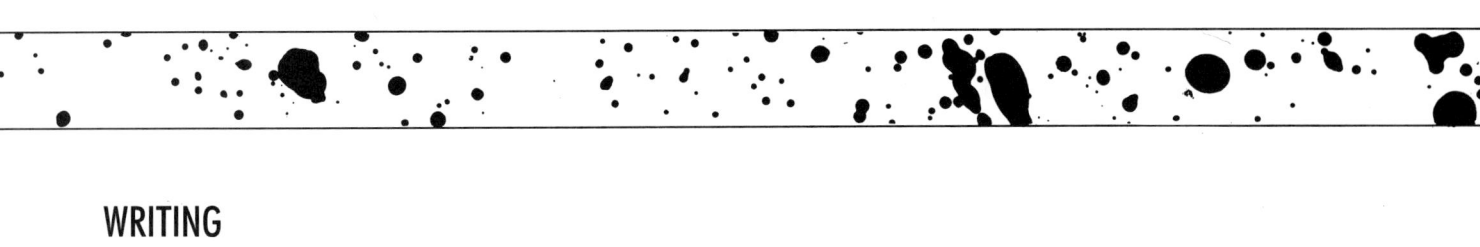

WRITING

Write a paragraph about a classmate or about yourself. Give the paragraph a title.

DISCUSSION TWO

With a partner, read your stories to each other. Take turns listening and reading. After you listen to your partner's story, ask him/her one question about the story.

EDITING

Correct this paragraph by adding capital letters and periods. Then rewrite it in its proper form.

the immigrant

alberto gomez came to the united states from mexico in 1984   he has been living and working in southern california since then   it was not easy for alberto to leave mexico   he discussed his plans with his parents before he came   he often receives letters in spanish from his family but alberto is lonely here

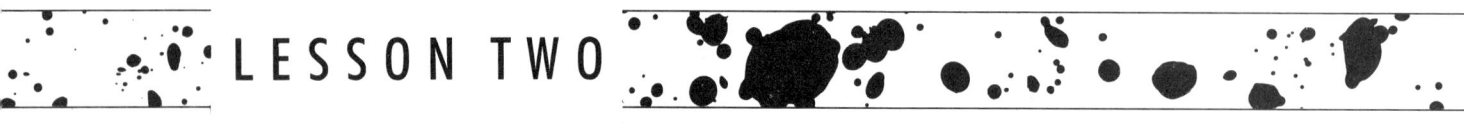

LESSON TWO

VOCABULARY

Verbs **Nouns**

decide decision
discuss discussion

Finish these sentences.

1. I have decided to _____.
2. We will discuss _____.
3. The decision _____.
4. This discussion _____.

DISCUSSION

Find a partner. Ask him/her these questions.

When did you come to the United States?
Did you come alone or with your family?
Was it a difficult decision to leave your country?

READING

Read this story twice, and talk about it with your teacher and classmates.

A Difficult Decision

Leaving her country was the most difficult decision of Mary Lam's life. Although she had an uncle in San Francisco, she had to leave the rest of her family in Taiwan, and she didn't know when she would see them again. Of course, being able to immigrate to the United States was a great chance for Mary, but she also knew that the streets of California were <u>not</u> made of gold. She knew that life would be difficult and lonely. She and her family discussed her plans. They discussed their ideas for several months and finally decided she should go. Everyone gave her money for the trip and to help start her new life. Her uncle said she could stay with him.

On the morning she left, it was raining and Mary woke up with tears in her eyes. Her mother and father were so old that she felt afraid to leave them. She worried that they would become sick or die and she would be too far away to help. She also worried that she would not be successful in her new life and would disappoint her family. She really didn't want her family to see her crying.

When she kissed her parents at the airport, she had a big smile on her face although her heart was breaking. Her mother was the last to say goodbye. "Always remember, my daughter," she said, "you may live anywhere in the world, but your home is where your heart is."

JOURNAL

Write your opinion. How did Mary feel about leaving her native country? Describe how you feel about leaving home.

_____
_____
_____
_____
_____
_____
_____
_____

EDITING

Unscramble these words to make sentences. Discard one word. The first one is done for you.

1. the to difficult make decide was very decision

    The decision was very difficult to make.

2. it about long time they a for discussed

    _____

3. immigration discussed discussion a family the about long had

    _____

4. passport get decision has to he decided a

    _____

LESSON THREE

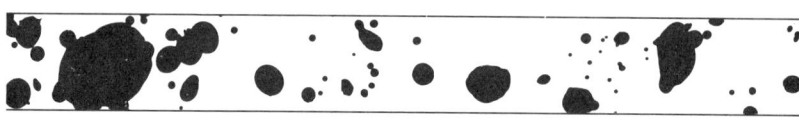

VOCABULARY

Adjectives

awful   helpful
painful   successful

Listen to the sentences your teacher dictates, and write them on the lines below.

1. _____
2. _____
3. _____
4. _____

DISCUSSION

In groups of three or four, give your classmates this information. Take turns listening and speaking.

In the first month that you lived in the United States, where did you live? What did you see? Where did you go? How did you feel?

EDITING

With a partner, read this letter and add correct punctuation.
Use capital letters, commas, and periods.

                                                                          nov 1   19XX

dear alex

    i've now been in the u s for two weeks and it's a very strange country   i can't read the street signs or the newspapers   everyone talks fast and i can't understand them   yesterday i got lost three times and i felt awful

    thank goodness for cousin sofia   she and her family have been very helpful to me   i share a room with sofia's six-year-old son ivan   they've also given me a job in their russian bakery   their business is very successful

    last weekend the family took me to visit some american friends   they gave us something

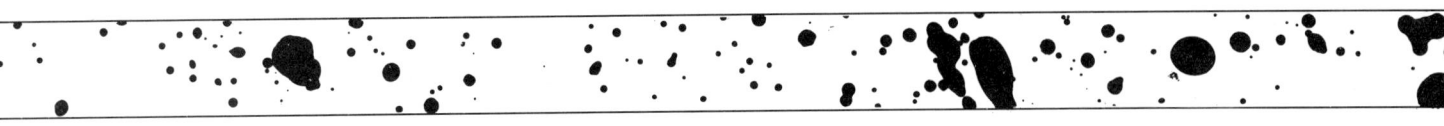

called chili   it was terrible   i couldn't eat it because it was too spicy   americans are strange people but they are friendly

i really miss everybody   it's painful to be far away from you and the rest of the family please write soon and tell me everything

love

Peter

WRITING ONE

Paraphrase the letter you just read by finishing these sentences.

Peter came from Russia _____.

He's living _____.

He thinks that the U.S. is _____.

He feels _____.

WRITING TWO

Write a paragraph about yourself. Describe your life in the United States.

_____
_____
_____
_____
_____
_____

UNIT 1 LOOKING AT ONESELF

LESSON FOUR

VOCABULARY

Adjectives

careful   hopeful
grateful   useful

Unscramble these words to make sentences. The first one is done for you.

1. careful very is Celia person a

   Celia is a very careful person.

2. because $50 gave he brother grateful his was him

   _____

3. apartment hopeful find I'm quiet I'll a

   _____

4. me useful gave my advice some friend

   _____

DISCUSSION ONE

With a partner, put the sentences in this paragraph in order. The first sentence is marked for you.

____ She finally found a place that looked convenient and inexpensive.

_1_   When Maria first came to Dallas, Texas, she lived with her brother and his family.

____ She has an appointment to meet the manager this evening, and she is hopeful that she can move soon.

____ The newspaper ads were useful and she called several places.

____ She was grateful for their help, but after their new baby was born, she decided to move.

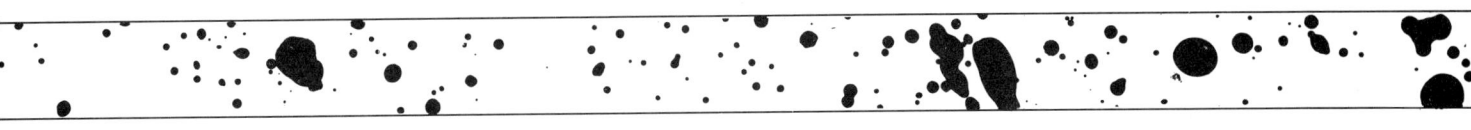

WRITING

Rewrite the paragraph from Discussion One in the correct form. Give the story a title.

DISCUSSION TWO

With a partner, check your writing for punctuation—periods, commas, capital letters, and indentation.

EDITING

Correct the grammar in these sentences. Each sentence has one mistake.

1. My family and I discussed about the trip to the United States.

2. He immigration here last year.

3. She was hope she could find a good job.

4. The apartment manager very helpful.

LESSON FIVE

VOCABULARY

Verbs	**Nouns**
apply	application
graduate	graduation

Fill in the blanks with words from the vocabulary list. Be sure that the verbs are in the correct tense.

1. His _____ is June 17.
2. He _____ to go to the National French Cooking School.
3. He _____ from high school before he went to France.
4. His _____ was accepted right away.

DISCUSSION

With a partner, put these pictures in order to make a story.

Picture # _____ _____
_____

Picture # _____ _____
_____

Picture # _____ _____
_____

Picture # _____ _____
_____

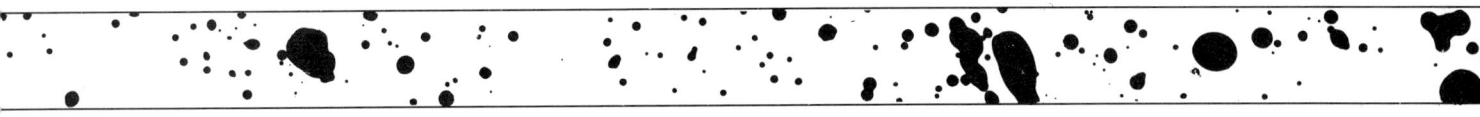

WRITING ONE

Listen to the teacher and write the sentences you hear below the appropriate picture on page 10.

WRITING TWO

Read this story and finish it. Add at least five sentences.

Studying in France

George Mason always wanted to have his own French restaurant. On his twenty-first birthday, he decided to go to Paris to study cooking.

_____

_____

_____

_____

_____

_____

_____

_____

_____

_____

_____

EDITING

Read this paragraph. Check the spelling of the underlined words. Correct the spelling if necessary.

After high school <u>graduation,</u> Suzanne <u>disided</u> to go to Japan to study art. She <u>aplyed</u> to an art school in Tokyo although she couldn't speak Japanese very well. She <u>dicsused</u> her plans with her parents, and they are going to give her the money because they want her to be <u>successfull.</u>

UNIT 1 LOOKING AT ONESELF

LESSON SIX

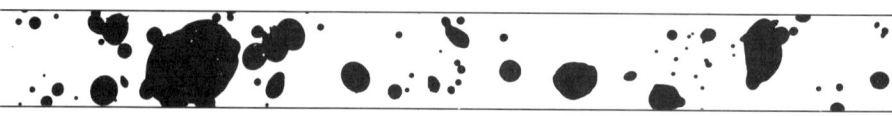

VOCABULARY

Verbs	Nouns	Adjectives
apply	application	awful
decide	decision	careful
describe	description	grateful
discuss	discussion	helpful
graduate	graduation	painful
immigrate	immigration	successful
		useful

Choose one noun, one verb, and one adjective, and write a sentence with each one.

1. _____
2. _____
3. _____

DISCUSSION ONE

Make a list of things you remember about your first few days in the United States. Choose the most interesting one and tell your partner about it. Take turns listening and speaking.

_____   _____
_____   _____
_____   _____

WRITING

Write about the most interesting thing you remember about your first few days in the United States.

<u>   *Memories*   </u>

_____
_____
_____
_____
_____
_____

DISCUSSION TWO

Read your story to a partner and listen to his/her story. Tell your partner one interesting thing you heard, and ask at least two questions about the story.

EDITING

Correct the grammar in these sentences. Each sentence has one mistake.

1. He is success in his business.

2. She description her country very well.

3. He applied about a visa for the United States.

4. Their discuss was about money.

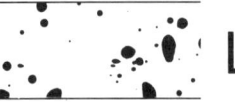 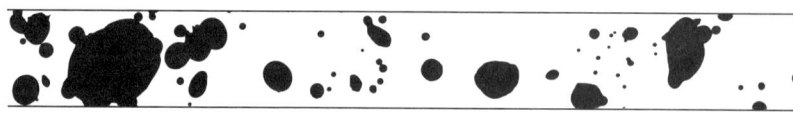

LESSON SEVEN

VOCABULARY

Connecting Words

and   but   because

Combine the two sentences to make one longer sentence. Use a connecting word from the vocabulary list.

1. I like this country. I don't speak English well.

2. She writes a lot of letters. She misses her friends in Peru.

3. He lives with his wife. He lives with his mother, too.

DISCUSSION

With a partner, read again the stories you wrote in Lesson Six. Check your stories for spelling and punctuation. Help each other to add at least three sentences to your stories. Use at least two connecting words.

WRITING

Rewrite your story in its new form. Give it a new title.

EDITING

Are these complete sentences? Mark each one *yes* or *no*. If it is not a complete sentence, rewrite it to make it complete.

_____ 1. And she filled out the application for the visa.

_____ 2. Because he had friends, he was happy.

_____ 3. But they were finally successful.

_____ 4. Because I didn't speak English.

LESSON EIGHT

Q·U·I·Z

I. VOCABULARY

Read the story. Choose the correct words and (circle) the answers.

My Country

I can (1) describe / (2) description / (3) described many things about my country. In the spring there are many beautiful flowers (1) and / (2) but / (3) because everyone feels happy. The winter weather is rainy and (1) grateful. / (2) hopeful. / (3) awful. In summer, the weather is hot and many people make a (1) decide / (2) decision / (3) decided to go to the beach, but it is always crowded. My favorite season is fall (1) and / (2) but / (3) because the weather is perfect and the fishing is good. You should visit my country soon, but don't forget to

(1) apply
(2) application   for a visa.
(3) applied

II. EDITING ONE

Correct this paragraph by adding periods, commas, and capital letters.

immigration

when i first came to the united states i was lonely and nervous   there were many things i didn't understand because i couldn't speak english   i feel much better in my new home now   i have some friends here but i still miss my family

III. EDITING TWO

Combine the two sentences to make one longer sentence. Use connecting words.

1. He studies English. He wants to get a job.

_____

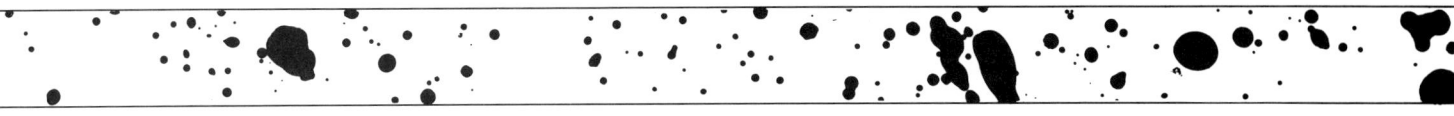

2. She likes American food. She doesn't know how to cook it.

   _____

3. They decided to move. Their apartment was too small.

   _____

4. I am from Mexico. I speak Spanish.

   _____

IV. WRITING

Write a story about this picture. Give the story a title.

_____

_____
_____
_____
_____
_____
_____
_____
_____

UNIT II
TALKING ABOUT EDUCATION

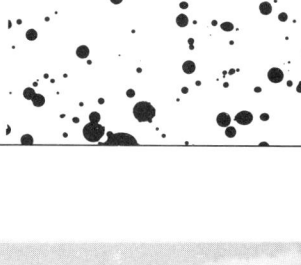

LESSON NINE

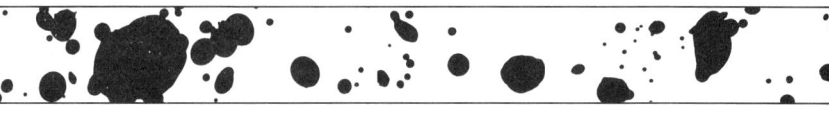

VOCABULARY

Verbs	**Nouns**
enroll	enrollment
require	requirement

Fill in the blanks with the words from the vocabulary list. Be sure the verbs are in the correct tense.

1. He _____ in school to learn English.
2. For this school, the only _____ is to be over 18.
3. Most jobs in the United States _____ English.
4. Our school has a very large _____.

DISCUSSION ONE

With a partner, make a list of things you *like* and *dislike* about school.

Like	**Dislike**
_____	_____
_____	_____
_____	_____
_____	_____

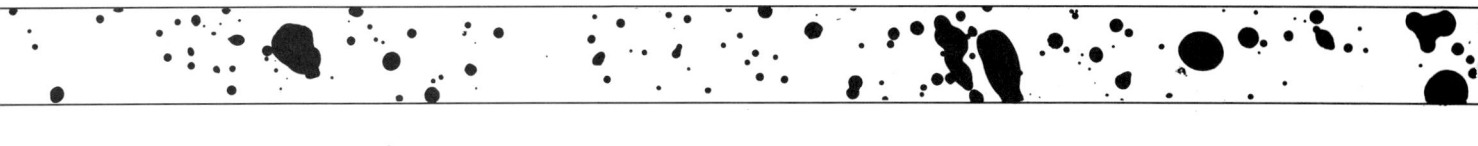

WRITING

Write a story about school. Give it a title.

_____

_____
_____
_____
_____
_____
_____
_____
_____
_____
_____
_____
_____

DISCUSSION TWO

Read your story to a partner and listen to his/her story.
After you listen to your partner's story, ask one question about it.

EDITING

The verbs in this story are in the wrong form. Correct them.

American Schools

In the United States, all children can enrolls in school for free. The law require everyone to go to school until age 16, but most people graduates from high school at 18. After 18, people can enrolled in adult school, community college, or a four-year college or university. Most adult schools or community colleges is free or inexpensive, but many colleges and universities were expensive.

LESSON TEN

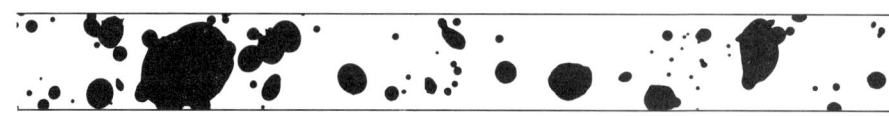

VOCABULARY

Adjectives

pleased   displeased
satisfied   dissatisfied

Unscramble these words to make sentences.

1. test pleased passed the he because was he
   _____

2. dissatisfied schedule her she class with was
   _____

3. teacher students because displeased late were the arrived the
   _____

4. work director her satisfied was with the
   _____

DISCUSSION

In groups of three, explain to your classmates why you enrolled in school. Take turns listening and speaking.

READING

Read this letter twice, and talk about it with your teacher and classmates.

September 20, 19XX

Dear Kevin,
    It's hard to believe that you are in your final year of high school. How time flies! I remember when you were born. I'm very pleased because you've grown up to be a fine young man.
    At this time in your life, you must make many important decisions, and I know that you probably feel confused. If you decide to do the wrong thing now, you may pay for your mistakes the rest of your life. Now, more than ever, you must put education first because it is the key to a successful future. Getting a good job usually requires having a good educational background.
    When I first came to the United States, I didn't have a high-school diploma. I was lucky. I had the opportunity to enroll in an adult school to learn English and finish high school. Because I got a high-school diploma, I had more opportunities for advancement. Nowadays, a college education is the basic requirement for a good job.

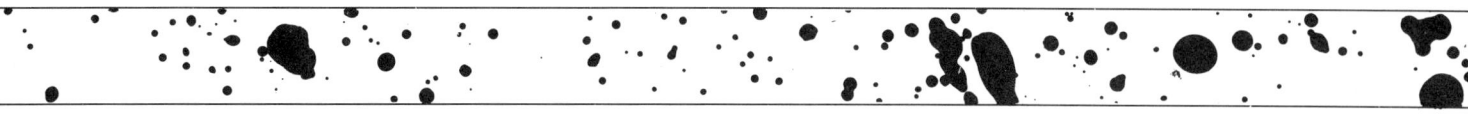

Kevin, you are an intelligent young man so I'm sure you'll make the right choices. There are several good universities in your state, but they are expensive. Your local community college would allow you more time to think about your future. Of course, you are welcome to come and stay with me and go to college here in Florida.

Whatever you choose, I hope you will not be dissatisfied. I wish you all the best. Please write soon.

Love,
Grandpa

JOURNAL

Write your opinion. Do you agree with the advice that Kevin's grandfather gave him? Do you think that a college education is necessary for advancement? Why or why not?

_____
_____
_____
_____
_____
_____
_____
_____
_____

EDITING

Correct this letter by adding capital letters, commas, periods, and apostrophes.

september 8   19XX

dear grandma

   i ve taken your advice and enrolled in an english class   i was nervous at first because i had to take a test   this is a school requirement and many of us took the test at the same time   i like my class but it s large   i ve already made two friends--one from vietnam and one from nicaragua   please write soon

love
lisa

UNIT II TALKING ABOUT EDUCATION

LESSON ELEVEN

VOCABULARY

Verbs **Nouns**

assign assignment
improve improvement

Answer these questions in complete sentences.

1. What do you need to improve?
   _____

2. When does your teacher assign homework?
   _____

DISCUSSION

Find a partner. Ask him/her about school.

Tell me about your first day of school here or in your country.
How did you feel? How old were you? Where were you?

EDITING

With a partner, read this story and add correct punctuation. Use periods, commas, apostrophes, and capital letters.

the first day

the first day of school can be very scary because everything is new and you don t know anybody it s easy to get lost in a strange building and it s terrible to be late on the first day

i remember my first day of english class in the united states i was very nervous and i got lost i couldn t ask directions because i didn t speak english when i finally found the classroom the teacher was talking and I was late

i sat in the back and took notes but i didn t enjoy myself because i was scared i couldn t

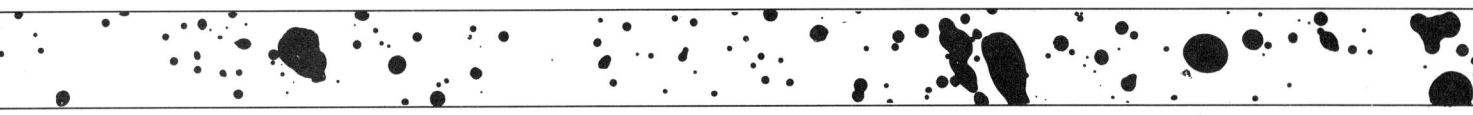

see the chalk board because the man in front of me was very tall   the teacher gave us an assignment but i didn t understand it   i was really disappointed

then the woman next to me explained what the teacher said   she was very helpful   by the end of the day i got to know some of my classmates and i felt much better   now i m pleased with my class and i think that school is a great place to meet people and make friends

WRITING ONE

Paraphrase the story you just read by finishing these sentences.

On the first day of school I was scared because _____
_____. I arrived late and
_____. The teacher wrote an assignment
on the chalk board but _____.
One of my classmates _____. Now I
think _____.

WRITING TWO

Write a story. Tell some things that happened to you on the first day of school.

My First Day of School

_____
_____
_____
_____
_____
_____
_____

LESSON TWELVE

Adjectives

bored   disappointed
confused   excited

Finish these sentences.

1. I was confused because _____.

2. My sister was disappointed because _____.

3. I felt bored because _____.

4. He was excited because _____.

DISCUSSION ONE

With a partner, put the sentences in this paragraph in order.

_____ The counselor suggested she enroll in nursing courses.

_____ When Julia first came to the United States, she was confused about her future.

_____ After Julia graduates next year, she will be a nurse.

_____ She talked to a counselor because she couldn't decide what to study.

_____ She wanted to go to college because she knew education was important.

WRITING

Add one sentence to the story in Discussion One. Rewrite it in its correct form, and give it a title.

_____

_____

_____

_____

_____

DISCUSSION TWO

With a partner, check your papers for punctuation—periods, commas, capital letters, and indentation.

EDITING

Correct this paragraph by adding capital letters, periods, commas, and question marks. Then rewrite it in its correct form.

    how does a student know which english class to take   to enroll in the correct class   the student must first see a counselor and take a test   usually the test is grammar and reading but some schools require a writing sample   then the counselor will ask questions and assign the correct classes

LESSON THIRTEEN

VOCABULARY

Verbs	**Nouns**
develop	development
encourage	encouragement

Listen to the sentences your teacher dictates, and write them on the lines below.

1. _____
2. _____
3. _____
4. _____

DISCUSSION ONE

With a partner, decide what each person is studying in these pictures.
Write one sentence about each picture.

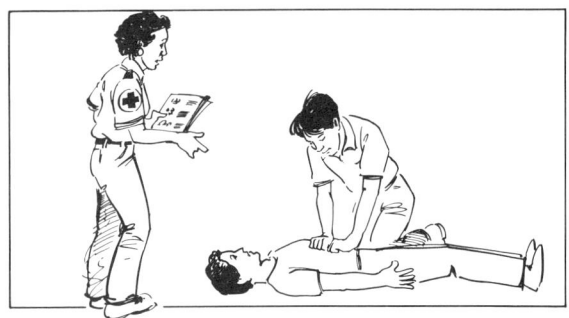

_____

_____

_____

_____

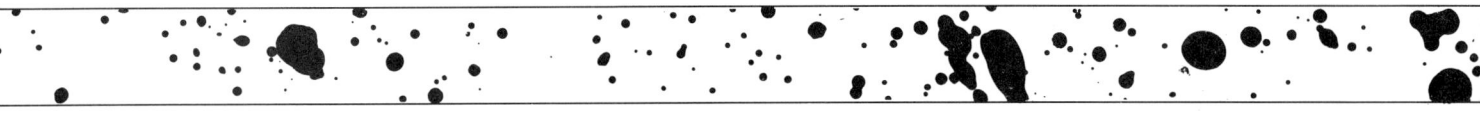

DISCUSSION TWO

Tell your partner what you would like to study after you learn English. Why?

WRITING

Read this story and finish it. Add at least six sentences. Give your story a title.

_____

Olga was tired of working as a waitress. The hours were bad, the work was hard, and the pay was terrible. She decided to go back to school, but she didn't know what to study. She made an appointment with a counselor and talked to him last week. He encouraged her to _____

_____
_____
_____
_____
_____
_____
_____
_____
_____
_____

EDITING

Read this story. Check the spelling of the underlined words. Correct the spelling if necessary.

Tests

Mark has decided to <u>enrole</u> at State University next semester, but he must pass the TOEFL first. English is a <u>requirement</u> for the university. He's taking a special English class now to <u>inprove</u> his English. The teacher would like him to <u>develope</u> his writing skills, and Mark agrees. He doesn't want to be <u>dissapionted</u> with his test scores, so he studies hard.

LESSON FOURTEEN

VOCABULARY

Verbs	Nouns	Adjectives
assign	assignment	bored
develop	development	confused
encourage	encouragement	disappointed
enroll	enrollment	displeased
improve	improvement	dissatisfied
require	requirement	excited
		pleased
		satisfied

Choose one verb, one noun, and one adjective, and write a sentence with each one.

1. _____
2. _____
3. _____

DISCUSSION ONE

Make a list of important things that parents should tell or teach their children. Read your list to a partner and explain it. Take turns listening and speaking.

_____   _____
_____   _____
_____   _____

WRITING

Your friend has a teenage child and needs some advice. Write a letter to your friend explaining how to be a good parent.

_____
_____
_____
_____
_____
_____

DISCUSSION TWO

Read your letter to a partner and listen to his/her letter. Tell your partner one interesting thing you heard, and ask at least two questions about the letter.

EDITING

Correct the grammar in these sentences. Each sentence has one mistake.

1. This school requirement students to take an English test.

2. He wants to get a good job because he has to learn English.

3. This class has helped me to make a lot of improve in my writing.

4. I was confuse about the grammar.

LESSON FIFTEEN

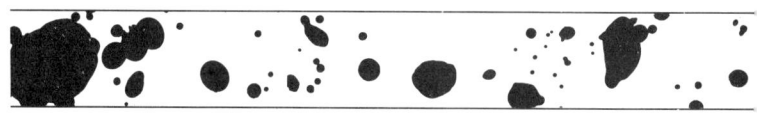

VOCABULARY

Connecting Words

although   and   because

Combine the two sentences to make one longer sentence. Use a connecting word from the vocabulary list.

1. He enjoyed his classes. They were difficult.
   _____

2. She enrolled in school. She wanted to improve her English.
   _____

3. Last week Maria saw the school counselor. He advised her to enroll in an accounting class.
   _____
   _____

4. I want to get a job soon. I have to graduate first.
   _____

DISCUSSION

With a partner, read the letters again that you wrote in Lesson Fourteen. Check each other's spelling and punctuation. Help each other to add at least three sentences to your letters. Use at least two connecting words.

WRITING

Rewrite your letter in its new form. Change the date.

EDITING

Are these complete sentences? Mark each one *yes* or *no*. If it is not a complete sentence, rewrite it to make it complete.

_____ 1. Although he was a good student.

_____ 2. Because he studied, he passed.

_____ 3. Because he wanted to take a computer class.

_____ 4. And she discussed it with the counselor.

LESSON SIXTEEN

Q·U·I·Z

I. VOCABULARY

Read the story. Choose the correct words and circle the answers.

October 7, 19XX

Dear Uncle Joe,

I am very (1) excited (2) excitement (3) exciting about my classes this semester. I (1) enrolling (2) enrolled (3) enrollment in a math class and two English classes. I'll take computer science next semester. Math is a (1) required (2) requiring (3) requirement for taking computer science. My English is (1) improve (2) improvement (3) improving every day (1) although (2) because (3) but my roommate is helping me. He gives me advice on vocabulary and now I don't feel so (1) confused. (2) confuse. (3) confusing. Are you coming to visit soon? I'd love to see you.

Love,

Joey

II. EDITING ONE

The verbs in this paragraph are in the wrong form. Correct them.

Lucy has recently enroll in a business college. She went to class four nights a week because she wanting to improved her job skills. She would likes to learn about computers, but the school require everyone to take a typing test. She can only typing in Spanish. She has decide to typed all of her assignments for more practice.

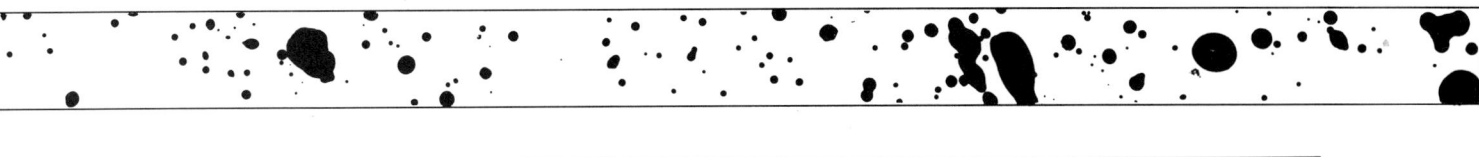

III. EDITING TWO

Are these complete sentences? Mark each one *yes* or *no*. If it is not a complete sentence, rewrite it to make it complete.

_____ 1. Although he did not understand the teacher.

_____ 2. Because he wants to work in a bank, he will study computer science.

_____ 3. Because education is important to him and his family.

_____ 4. Although he has not yet finished his homework.

_____ 5. But I would like to enroll in a good school nearby.

IV. WRITING

Read this letter from Jose. On a separate piece of paper, answer it and give him some good advice.

January 3, 19XX

Dear Friend,

    I'm writing this letter to you because I'm confused and I need some advice. I'm going to move to the United States soon, but I'm very nervous. I don't speak English and I'm worried about that. Is English a requirement for work? I don't have much money so I need to learn quickly. What is the best way to learn English? What should I do?

    Please write soon.

Your friend,

Jose

UNIT III
THINKING ABOUT JOBS

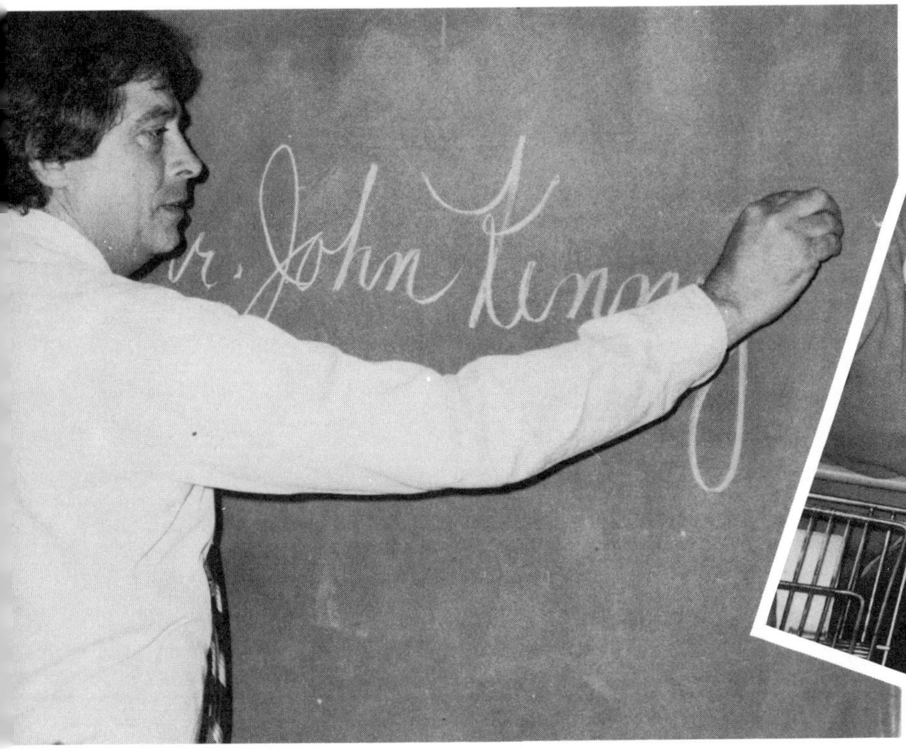

LESSON SEVENTEEN

VOCABULARY

Adjectives

competent   incompetent
convenient   inconvenient

Listen to the sentences your teacher dictates, and write them on the lines below.

1. _____

2. _____

3. _____

4. _____

DISCUSSION ONE

With a partner, make two lists. Write three things you *should* do and three things you *shouldn't* do at a job interview.

Should	Shouldn't
_____	_____
_____	_____
_____	_____

WRITING

Read this story and finish it. Add at least six sentences. Give the story a title.

If you want to get a job, there are several things you should and shouldn't do.

DISCUSSION TWO

Read your story to a partner and listen to his/her story. After you listen to your partner's story, ask one question about getting a job.

EDITING

The verbs in this paragraph are in the wrong form. Correct them.

Employment in the U.S.A.

Many people in the United States gets jobs by going to an employment agency. You should made an appointment with a job counselor at a convenient time. Before your appointment, you must taking a test. The test showed what you were competent to do. The counselor will tells you about job openings. You should asking who have to pay the agency for the job.

LESSON EIGHTEEN

VOCABULARY

Adjectives

confused   confusing
disappointed   disappointing

Answer these questions in complete sentences.

1. Why do you sometimes feel confused?
   _____

2. What is confusing to you?
   _____

3. When do you feel disappointed?
   _____

4. What is disappointing to you?
   _____

DISCUSSION

In groups of three or four, discuss finding jobs in the United States. Give your classmates this information. Take turns listening and speaking.

Have you ever looked for a job in the United States? Is it easy or difficult to find one here? Why?

READING

Read this article twice, and talk about it with your teacher and classmates.

Education is the Key to Job Success Today

Economists often tell us that there are many, many jobs available. Although most people agree that this is true, a high-school dropout is often disappointed in his/her job search. These facts are confusing to most of us.

The reason we are confused is that the job market is changing rapidly. Before the age of computers, many jobs did not require a lot of training and education. Since the 1970s, more and more jobs have required technical skills.

There are twelve million <u>new</u> jobs in the United States today that were not available in 1982, but many of them require some college education or technical training. This educational requirement will probably become greater in the future.

Before the year 2000, the United States government thinks there will be about a 75% growth in health-care jobs. These jobs need trained, competent workers.

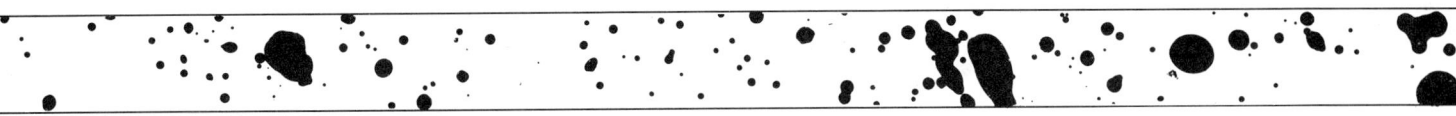

At the same time, jobs that require less training are disappearing. For example, by the year 2000, there will be 25% fewer farm jobs and 54% fewer electronic-assembler jobs.

"The key to economic success will be making the correct educational choices," said Professor Glen Simpson. "If people do not choose to get more and better education, they will not succeed."

JOURNAL

Write your opinion. How do you feel about the changing job market? Will it be easier or more difficult for you to find a job in the future? Why?

_____
_____
_____
_____
_____
_____
_____
_____

WHERE THE JOBS ARE	
Ten Fastest-Growing Occupations	Changes 1984 - 1985
Paralegal personnel	104%
Medical assistants	90%
Physical therapist assistants	82%
Data-processing equipment repairers	80%
Home health aides	80%
Computer systems analysts	76%
Medical record technicians	75%
Employment interviewers	71%
Computer programmers	70%
Radiology technologists/ technicians	65%
...and Four Occupations That Will Lose Jobs	
Electrical electronic assemblers	54%
Industrial truck/tractor operators	34%
Stenographers	28%
Farmers, farm workers	28%

This chart shows where the jobs will be in the future. It shows the percent of growth (or loss) that we can expect between now and the year 2000. *(Dept. of Labor Statistics)*

EDITING

Unscramble these words to make sentences. Discard one word.

1. disappointed job didn't disappointing was he because he the get

   _____

2. a to must to get these job you competent very be days

   _____

3. confused supervisor instructions confusing us gave the very

   _____

4. location take inconvenient was decided job to he the because the convenient

   _____

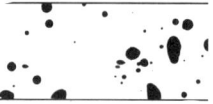 # LESSON NINETEEN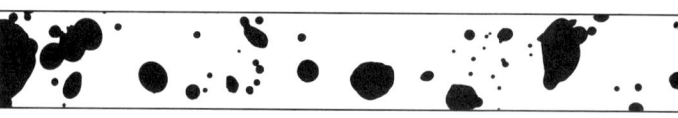

VOCABULARY

Adjectives

absent   current
confident   recent

Finish these sentences.

1. He was absent because _____.
2. Although she felt confident _____.
3. He likes his current job but _____.
4. Her most recent work experience was _____.

DISCUSSION

In groups of three, discuss things you should include in a letter when you apply for a job. Make a list.

_____   _____

_____   _____

_____   _____

EDITING

With a partner, read this business letter and add correct punctuation.
Use periods, commas, apostrophes, and capital letters. Circle the colon.

ms   maggie o'brien   921 myrtle st   s e

personnel manager   seattle   wa   98155

first state bank   september 2   19xx

1754--3rd ave   n w

seattle   wa   98102

dear ms   o'brien:

    i would like to apply for the computer programming job that you advertised in the sunday <u>seattle times</u>   i have just completed my third class in computer programming at northwest business college and have been working part-time as a computer programmer at

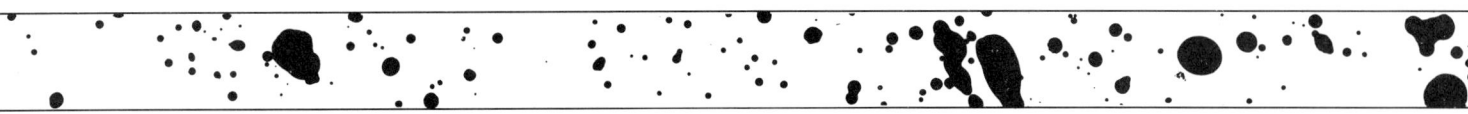

school   my recent work experience as a clerk typist for an insurance company has helped me to become a competent computer operator   my educational background in math has made programming easier   i m confident that i can do a good job for the bank because i have good training and work experience

i m available for an interview any afternoon   i am including a job application and a list of references

if you need more information please do not hesitate to call

sincerely
Mary Jane Alioto

WRITING ONE

Paraphrase the letter you just read by finishing these sentences.

Mary Jane Alioto wrote to Ms. O'Brien because _____
_____. Although she doesn't have a lot of experience as a computer programmer, she _____
_____. She feels confident she can do a good job because _____. If Ms. O'Brien needs more information, she can _____.

WRITING TWO

Write a paragraph. Tell about a job you have had.

_____
_____
_____
_____
_____

LESSON TWENTY

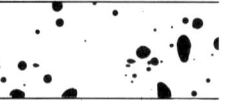
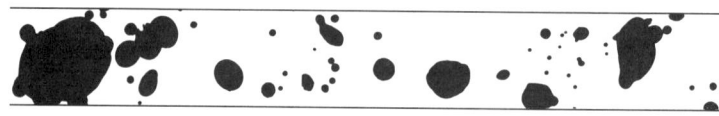

VOCABULARY

Adjectives

bored	boring
excited	exciting
frustrated	frustrating
interested	interesting

Fill in the blanks with words from the vocabulary list.

1. I left because the movie was _____.
2. When she feels _____, she always asks for help.
3. He was very _____ because he got a new job.
4. The job was _____, but the pay was terrible.

DISCUSSION ONE

With a partner, read the story and put the sentences in the second paragraph in order.

An Exciting New Job

Judy Olsen has just gotten an interesting new job because her old one was boring. She's excited about this new job because she'll earn more money, but she's worried that it might be confusing. She is a maid in a very large and expensive hotel. She's afraid she might get lost.

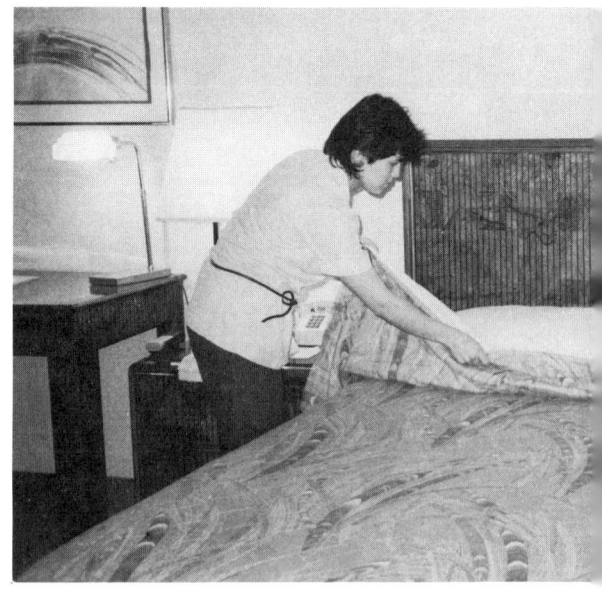

_1_ On the first day, the boss left her a note to explain the job. He wrote down many things.

____ When you enter the room, remove all the sheets and towels whether they are dirty or not.

____ Give everything a final check and be sure the door is locked when you leave.

____ Put on your uniform and go to the top floor.

____ Vacuum the carpets and clean the tub and toilet before you put in the clean linen.

____ Check every room without a "Do Not Disturb" sign.

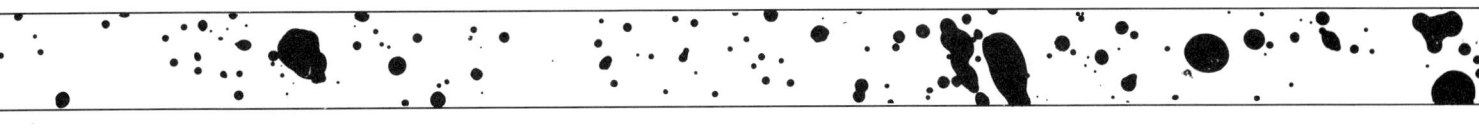

WRITING

Add one sentence to the second paragraph in Discussion One. Rewrite it in its correct form.

_____
_____
_____
_____
_____
_____
_____
_____
_____
_____
_____
_____
_____
_____

DISCUSSION TWO

With a partner, check your papers for punctuation—capital letters, periods, commas, and indentation.

EDITING

Correct this paragraph by adding capital letters, periods, commas, and apostrophes. Then rewrite it in its correct form on a separate piece of paper.

louis used to work as a janitor in a bank   he didn t like the job very much because the hours were terrible   although the pay was good   he decided to look for a new job   his friend told him that the post office needed clerks   he passed the test and had an interview   he got the job and he likes it

UNIT III THINKING ABOUT JOBS

LESSON TWENTY-ONE

VOCABULARY

Adjectives

dependent   independent
efficient   inefficient

Unscramble these words to make sentences.

1. because efficient the likes is Jason boss he

2. worker fired she an was got inefficient she because

3. transportation is George for dependent bus the on

4. independent a Mary job feels because has she

DISCUSSION

With a partner, put these pictures in order to make a story. Write one sentence about each picture.

Picture # _____   _____

Picture # _____   _____

Picture # _____   _____

Picture # _____   _____

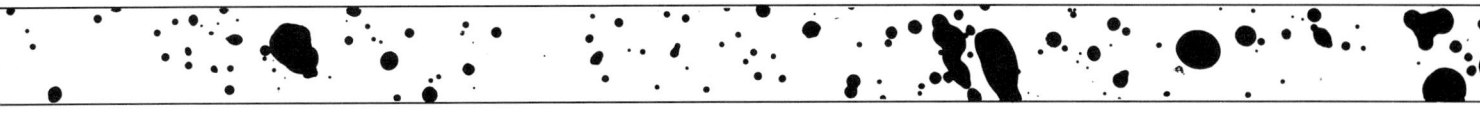

WRITING ONE

Listen to the teacher and take some notes. Write the important details in the correct column.

TED	CAROLE

WRITING TWO

Use your notes to write a story. Give it a title.

_____

_____
_____
_____
_____
_____
_____
_____
_____
_____
_____

EDITING

Read this paragraph. Check the spelling of the underlined words. Correct the spelling if necessary.

    Jack is <u>disapionted</u> because his job is so boring. He has been looking for another job.

He'd like to find one that is more <u>exiting</u> and in a more <u>conveint</u> place. He is <u>confident</u> that

he will find one soon. Someone will hire him because he is an <u>eficent</u> worker.

LESSON TWENTY-TWO

VOCABULARY

Adjectives

absent	current	frustrating
bored	dependent	incompetent
boring	disappointed	inconvenient
competent	disappointing	independent
confident	efficient	inefficient
confused	excited	interested
confusing	exciting	interesting
convenient	frustrated	recent

Choose four adjectives and write sentences with each one.

1. _____
2. _____
3. _____
4. _____

DISCUSSION ONE

With a partner, make a list of the things you need to do to get a job. Then, put the list in order. What should you do first, second, third?

WRITING

Write at least two paragraphs. Explain how to get a job. Tell what you should do before the interview. Then tell what you should do at the interview. Give your story a title.

DISCUSSION TWO

Read your story to a partner and listen to his/her story. Tell your partner two interesting things you heard, and ask at least two questions about the story.

EDITING

Correct this letter by adding capital letters, periods, commas, and colons.

mr   russell wilkins   1776 a   washington st
manager   a-1 insurance co   boston   ma
12 north church st
boston   ma   july 4   19XX

dear mr   wilkins

   thank you for your letter   i will be happy to come for an interview on july 14 at 1 30 p m

   sincerely
   Francis Baron
   francis baron

UNIT III THINKING ABOUT JOBS

LESSON TWENTY-THREE

VOCABULARY

Connecting Words

after   because
although   before

Combine the two sentences to make one longer sentence. Use a connecting word from the vocabulary list.

1. He wanted to get a new job. His old job was boring.

2. He read the ads every day. He couldn't understand them.

3. She dressed carefully. She went to the interview.

4. She mailed the letter. She typed the letter.

DISCUSSION

With a partner, read the stories again that you wrote in Lesson Twenty-Two. Check each other's spelling and punctuation. Help each other to add at least three sentences to your stories. Use at least three connecting words.

WRITING

Rewrite your story in its new form. Give it a new title.

EDITING

Are these complete sentences? Mark each one *yes* or *no*. If it is not a complete sentence, rewrite it to make it complete.

_____ 1. Because she didn't have a job, she was looking for one.

_____ 2. He went to the interview after.

_____ 3. Before he caught the bus on the corner next to his house.

_____ 4. Although she didn't have any experience as a computer programmer.

LESSON TWENTY-FOUR

Q·U·I·Z

I. VOCABULARY

Read the story. Choose the correct words and circle the answers.

Alice is very (1) boring (2) bored (3) boredom because she isn't working now. She was a cashier in a busy restaurant. However, she only had the job for three days. On the first night, she couldn't work the cash register because it was different. The boss explained it to her very quickly but she still felt (1) confused. (2) confusing. (3) confusion. She didn't think it was (1) interested (2) competent (3) important to ask him again, so she made a lot of mistakes. The boss got angry with her. The next day she didn't feel very (1) confident, (2) absent, (3) convenient, so she came late. She made more mistakes (1) before (2) although (3) because she was nervous. The next day Alice didn't come to work at all, so the boss fired her. She feels very (1) disappointing. (2) disappointed. (3) dependent.

II. EDITING ONE

Unscramble these words to make sentences. Discard one word.

1. the didn't after speak before to English came I United States I
   _____

2. she Tina although job needed her money quit but
   _____

3. was the called when exciting manager Pete very him excited
   _____

4. incompetent because she job got the competent was she
   _____

52   THE WRITING CHALLENGE

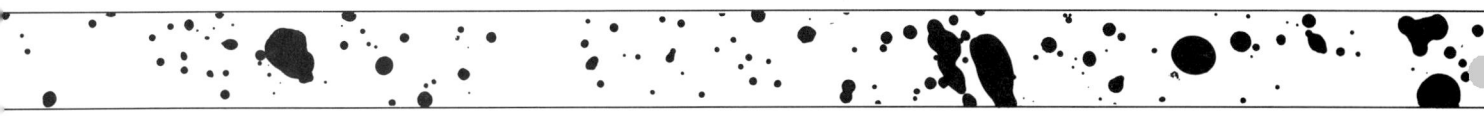

III. EDITING TWO

Read this story. Check the spelling of the underlined words. Correct the spelling if necessary.

If you want to get a job, there are several things you should do. It's <u>improtant</u> to look in the newspaper every day <u>althought</u> it is difficult to read the ads. You need to be <u>pateint</u> to find a job. When you find an <u>intresting</u> job ad, you should find out the <u>requirements</u>. When you go to an interview, you should dress carefully and be on time. Be polite and <u>confiant</u>.

IV. WRITING

Larry Lee has just gotten a job in a restaurant. He likes the job and he needs the money. Write a letter to Larry. Tell him how to be successful on his new job.

UNIT IV
DESCRIBING SOCIAL CUSTOMS

LESSON TWENTY-FIVE

VOCABULARY

Verbs	**Nouns**
celebrate	celebration
invite	invitation

Answer these questions in complete sentences.

1. What holidays do you usually celebrate?
   _____

2. Who would you like to invite to your birthday party?
   _____

3. What is your favorite celebration?
   _____

4. What should you do when you get an invitation?
   _____

DISCUSSION ONE

With a partner, make a list of adjectives about these people.

_____
_____
_____
_____
_____
_____

WRITING

Read this story and finish it. Add at least seven sentences. Give the story a title.

_____

Laurie and Jack got married when they were 22 years old. They had a beautiful church wedding and invited many people to the celebration.

_____

DISCUSSION TWO

Read your story to a partner and listen to his/her story. After you listen to your partner's story, ask one question about Jack and Laurie.

EDITING

Correct this story by adding capital letters, periods, commas, and apostrophes. Then rewrite it in its correct form on a separate piece of paper.

wedding plans

sue and bill have many things to do before they get married next week   although their wedding will be in a church   they must get a marriage license from the state   they re going to city hall this afternoon to get it   tomorrow sue has to pick up her dress and bill has to pick up the wedding rings   they also have to order a lot of food because they have invited a lot of people to their celebration

LESSON TWENTY-SIX

VOCABULARY

Verbs	Adjectives
hurry	hurried
marry	married
worry	worried

Listen to the sentences your teacher dictates, and write them on the lines below.

1. _____
2. _____
3. _____
4. _____

DISCUSSION

In groups of three or four, give your classmates this information. Take turns listening and speaking.

At what age do people usually get married in your country? What kind of celebration do they have? If a husband and wife are not happy together, what do they do? Do many people in your country get married for a second time?

READING

Read this article twice, and talk about it with your teacher and classmates.

Marriage--American Style

Marriage is very important in every country, and it is usually a reason for a big celebration. In the United States there are many different kinds of weddings. Some wedding ceremonies are religious, and some are civil. Most weddings are in a church, at home, or in some special place. Everyone has different ideas about special places. Recently one couple got married in the air after they jumped out of an airplane!

Although people get married at all ages, the average age for American brides is 23½. The average age of grooms is 26. Because many teenage marriages end in divorce, worried parents encourage their children not to marry too young.

It is frightening to realize that almost 50% of all marriages in this country end in divorce. Most Americans worry that divorce has become too common. Although people may not agree on the reasons for divorce or how to improve a marriage, they agree it's a problem.

Most Americans prefer to be married, so they often marry a second time. Remarriage is common after a person has been divorced or widowed. The result of these new marriages is a new kind of American family. Children in these families often have step-brothers and step-sisters, half-brothers and half-sisters, and even two sets of parents.

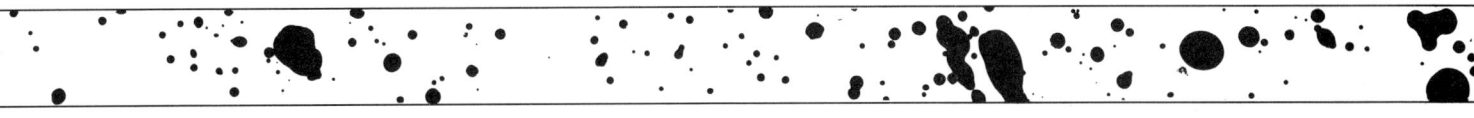

JOURNAL

Write your opinion. What do you think is the right age for a person to get married? Should married people get a divorce if they are not happy? Should people who are divorced or widowed get married again?

_____
_____
_____
_____
_____
_____
_____
_____
_____
_____
_____
_____

EDITING

Correct the grammar in these sentences. Each sentence has more than one mistake.

1. He will be get marry next month.
   _____

2. Jack will take Laurie go Hawaii for a honeymoon.
   _____

3. They will worried about their teenage daughter marriage.
   _____

4. Sue hurrying to prepared for her wedding.
   _____

UNIT IV DESCRIBING SOCIAL CUSTOMS

LESSON TWENTY-SEVEN

VOCABULARY

Verbs	Nouns
adjust	adjustment
disappoint	disappointment
retire	retirement

Unscramble these words to make sentences.

1. retired adjustment he he make big after had to a

   _____

2. supervisor she didn't her want disappoint to

   _____

3. his his he children schedule adjusted take care to of

   _____

4. her her her big co-workers retirement gave party for a

   _____

EDITING

With a partner, read this letter and add correct punctuation. Use capital letters, periods, apostrophes, commas, and question marks.

july 12   19XX

dear katherine

   your retirement party was wonderful   you re lucky to have such good friends   after working at american bank for 35 years   you ve made many friends   they love you   thanks for inviting me to the party   i had a marvelous time

   you said you were worried about retirement because there are so many adjustments to make   it s natural to worry about big changes in your life but retirement can be wonderful   although you ll miss your job and co-workers   you will find many new and exciting things to do   have you ever thought about painting   would you like to take a class   are you doing any volunteer work   there are hundreds of ways to enjoy your new freedom

THE WRITING CHALLENGE

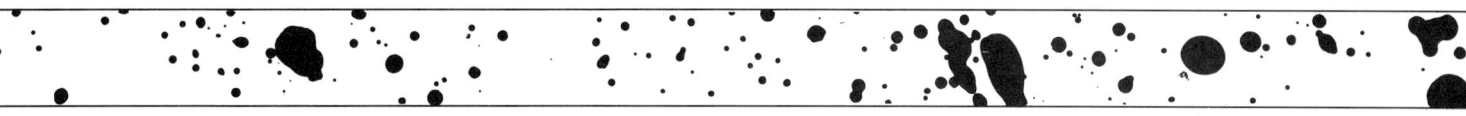

martha and i are going to take a cruise next september to celebrate our 40th wedding anniversary   why don t you come with us   we d love that and we ll be disappointed if you won t come   we ll celebrate your 66th birthday at the same time   after retirement you can travel any time you want to

write soon   i look forward to a long letter instead of your hurried notes

love
Stanley

WRITING ONE

Paraphrase the letter you just read by writing the missing sentences.

Stanley wrote to Katherine about her retirement from American Bank. _____

_____

Katherine was worried about all the adjustments she had to make. _____

_____

He also invited her to go on a cruise. _____

_____

DISCUSSION

Read your paraphrase to your partner and talk about it.

WRITING TWO

On a separate piece of paper, write a letter to your friend. Tell him/her how you celebrated your last birthday.

LESSON TWENTY-EIGHT

VOCABULARY

Verbs **Nouns**

announce   announcement
arrange   arrangement

Finish these sentences.

1. He arranged _____.

2. He made arrangements for _____.

3. She announced _____.

4. She made an announcement about _____.

DISCUSSION ONE

With a partner, read the story and put the sentences in the second and third paragraphs in order.

Bill will graduate from City College next month, and he has sent graduation announcements to his family and friends. After the graduation, his parents have arranged a celebration.

_____ After all guests have arrived, the students will march in and sit in front.

_____ The graduation will be in the auditorium of the school.

_____ When the school president announces each name, the student will stand up to get his/her diploma.

_____ All the graduating students will wear caps and gowns over their regular clothes.

_____ They will have a lot of food, some cake, and some champagne.

_____ After the graduation, Bill's friends will go to his parents' home for a party.

_____ Bill and his parents want everyone to have a good time.

_____ They have made arrangements for a band because young people like to dance.

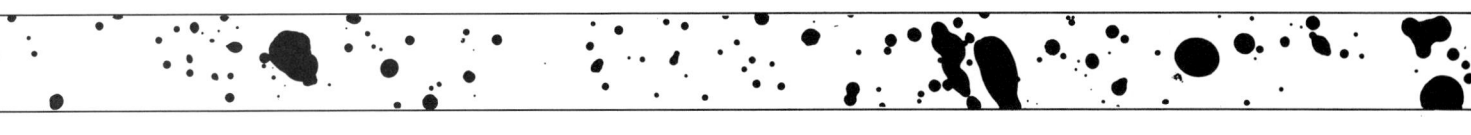

WRITING

Add one sentence to each paragraph in Discussion One. Rewrite the story in its correct form, and give it a title.

_____

_____
_____
_____
_____
_____
_____
_____
_____
_____
_____

DISCUSSION TWO

With a partner, check your papers for punctuation—capital letters, periods, commas, and indentation.

EDITING

Are these complete sentences? Mark each one *yes* or *no*. If it is not a complete sentence, rewrite it to make it complete.

_____ 1. Although she made arrangements to buy a graduation cake.

  _____

_____ 2. Because he had to work, he couldn't go to the party.

  _____

_____ 3. After they announced their wedding plans to their parents and sent their invitations to their friends.

  _____

_____ 4. Before Bill graduated from college.

  _____

LESSON TWENTY-NINE

VOCABULARY

Adjectives

beautiful   thankful
colorful   wonderful

Fill in the blanks with the words from the vocabulary list.

1. Although the dinner was _____, she couldn't eat it all.
2. He felt _____ because his son graduated from the university.
3. Her holiday dress was _____ but she only wore it once.
4. The fireworks were very _____ in the night sky.

DISCUSSION

With a partner write the date of each holiday shown in these pictures. Then write one sentence about each picture.

WRITING ONE

Listen to the teacher and take some notes. Write the important details in the correct column.

INDEPENDENCE DAY	HALLOWEEN	THANKSGIVING	CHRISTMAS

WRITING TWO

Use your notes to write one sentence about each holiday.

1. _____
2. _____
3. _____
4. _____

EDITING

Read this paragraph. Check the spelling of the underlined words. Correct the spelling if necessary.

Betty is sending out <u>invitions</u> to her Christmas party <u>althought</u> it's only the first of December. She's <u>worried</u> that people will be busy if she invites them too late. She has already bought some <u>beatiful</u> decorations for her house. She wanted to buy a red tablecloth, but they didn't have that <u>clor</u> at Sun's Department Store. She wasn't <u>dissapionted</u> because she already had a green one to use.

UNIT IV DESCRIBING SOCIAL CUSTOMS

LESSON THIRTY

VOCABULARY

Verbs	Adjectives	Nouns
adjust		adjustment
announce		announcement
arrange		arrangement
	beautiful	
celebrate		celebration
	colorful	
disappoint		disappointment
hurry	hurried	
invite		invitation
marry	married	
retire		retirement
	thankful	
	wonderful	
worry	worried	

Choose one verb, one adjective, and one noun, and write a sentence with each one.

1. _____
2. _____
3. _____

DISCUSSION ONE

In groups of two or three, tell about a holiday in your country. Take turns listening and speaking.

WRITING

Write at least two paragraphs. Describe a holiday in your country. Give your story a title.

DISCUSSION TWO

Read your story to a partner and listen to his/her story. Tell your partner two interesting things you heard, and ask at least two questions about the story.

EDITING

Unscramble these words to make sentences. Discard one word.

1. married next will the marry she in month church get

2. disappointment Christmas to couldn't because was party the go she disappointed Virginia

3. invited friends a party his invitation he his to Halloween at house

4. to party worried money wants a he's the worry he have but about

UNIT IV DESCRIBING SOCIAL CUSTOMS

LESSON THIRTY-ONE

VOCABULARY

Connecting Words

because   if
but   so

Combine these two sentences to make one longer sentence. Use a connecting word from the vocabulary list.

1. They will take a honeymoon. They will get married.
   _____

2. She's going to have a Christmas party. She likes to celebrate.
   _____

3. He'll probably eat a lot of food at Thanksgiving. He doesn't like turkey.
   _____

4. She wants to see the parade on the Fourth of July. She'll arrive early.
   _____

DISCUSSION

With a partner, read the story again that you wrote in Lesson Thirty. Check each other's spelling and punctuation. Help each other to add at least four sentences to your stories. Use at least three connecting words.

WRITING

Rewrite your story in its new form. Give it a new title.

_____

_____
_____
_____
_____
_____
_____
_____

EDITING

Are these complete sentences? Mark each one *yes* or *no*. If it is not a complete sentence, rewrite it to make it complete.

_____ 1. If she decides to have a party.

_____ 2. He wants to graduate so he has to study.

_____ 3. Because he was unhappy.

_____ 4. But they didn't send the invitations in time.

LESSON THIRTY-TWO

Q·U·I·Z

I. VOCABULARY

Read the story. Choose the correct words and circle the answers.

This year we're going to have a special Thanksgiving (1) celebrating. (2) celebrate. (3) celebration. We have

(1) invited
(2) inviting   all our brothers, sisters, aunts, uncles, cousins, and friends. My mother is
(3) invitation

excited, but she's (1) worry (2) worried (3) worries that we won't have enough dishes. We plan to

(1) arrangement
(2) arranging   three tables for everyone to sit at. We are
(3) arrange

(1) thanks
(2) thankful   that
(3) thank you

everyone can come, although we must (1) hurrying (2) hurried (3) hurry to get everything ready on time.

II. EDITING ONE

Correct this letter by adding capital letters, periods, commas, and apostrophes.

october 15   19XX

dear larry

   i ve just come back from bill and lisa s wedding   it was beautiful   lisa looked wonderful in her long white dress and bill looked handsome too

   i thought the reception was very nice but they were disappointed about it   they had to move the party inside because it started to rain   i had a great time but i had to leave early

   bill and lisa send their love

your brother
Harry

III. EDITING TWO

Correct the grammar in these sentences. Each sentence has more than one mistake.

1. John not go to the Christmas party because had working.

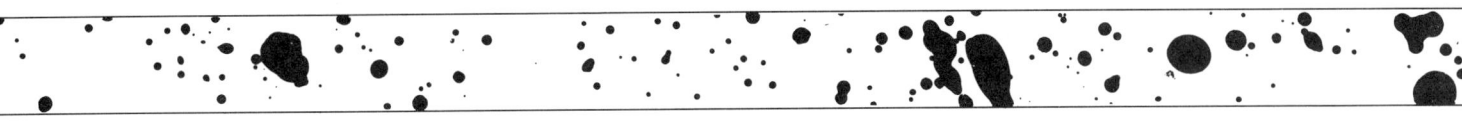

2. If they get marry, they will to invite a lot of people to the wedding.

3. The bride parents took care the arrangements for the wedding.

4. He was eat the turkey Thanksgiving and he like it.

IV. WRITING

Write a story about this picture.

UNIT V
MAKING TRAVEL PLANS

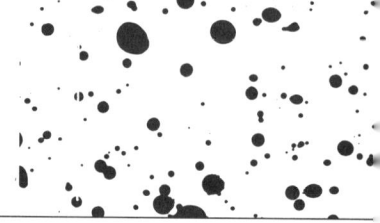

LESSON THIRTY-THREE

VOCABULARY

Adjectives

famous	gorgeous
glamorous	marvelous

Unscramble these words to make sentences.

1. one famous Golden Gate the is of Bridge San Francisco the in most places
   _____

2. very Nevada city a is Las Vegas in glamorous
   _____

3. marvelous wide River and the is it's Mississippi because long
   _____

4. mountains beaches Hawaii gorgeous has and beautiful
   _____

DISCUSSION

With a partner, make a list of adjectives about this picture.

_____
_____
_____
_____
_____
_____

WRITING ONE

Choose four adjectives from your list, and write sentences about the picture. Then read your sentences to your partner.

1. _____
2. _____

3. _____
4. _____

WRITING TWO

Read this story and finish it. Use several of the sentences you wrote about the picture. Give the story a title.

_____

I've always wanted to see New York City. _____

_____
_____
_____
_____
_____
_____
_____
_____
_____
_____
_____
_____

EDITING

Correct this story by adding capital letters, periods, commas, and apostrophes. Then rewrite it in its correct form on a separate piece of paper.

a marvelous vacation

last spring my friend and i took a trip to miami florida   we stayed at a glamorous hotel on the beach   because the weather was warm   we were able to walk on the beach early in the morning   every morning we saw a gorgeous sunrise   we didn t visit any famous places because we just wanted to relax on the beach   although we stayed in miami for two weeks   we weren t ready to return home

UNIT V MAKING TRAVEL PLANS

LESSON THIRTY-FOUR

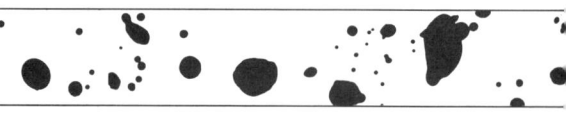

VOCABULARY

Adjectives	Nouns
happy	happiness
lonely	loneliness
sad	sadness

Answer these questions in complete sentences.

1. What makes you happy?
   _____

2. What can cause sadness?
   _____

3. Is loneliness healthy?
   _____

4. When do you feel lonely?
   _____

DISCUSSION

Find a partner. Ask him/her these questions.

How many countries have you lived in? How many have you visited?
Where did you live before you came here? Which continent?
How did you feel when you left your native country? Why?
How did you feel when you arrived here? Why? Was it a long journey?

READING

Read this letter twice, and talk about it with your teacher and classmates.

April 29, 1850
San Francisco

My Darling Wife Rebecca,

Today I finally arrived at the San Francisco Bay. You can imagine my happiness when I looked out from the ship and at last saw the town. My only sadness was that you were not beside me.

San Francisco isn't a very glamorous place. Most of the buildings are temporary and quite small. The only hotels are really ships that have been pulled up onto the beach.

The city is full of people who have come to find gold, but not everybody wants to work for it. There are many gamblers and other dangerous men who prefer to steal and kill.

There are very few women and children in this town because the journey by sea or across the continent is so difficult. I can't believe some people walked all the way from the

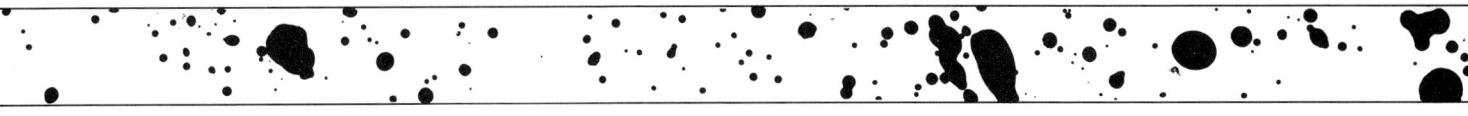

Mississippi River to the Pacific Ocean. Every day my heart is full of thankfulness that I made the journey by sea safely.

My thoughts are with you and the children always. My loneliness is sometimes so great that I don't know what to do. However, I'm sure my decision to come was correct. I know I will find gold and return home within a year.

I send my love. Take care of yourself and our precious children.   Your devoted husband,

Joseph

JOURNAL

Write your opinion. Why do you think Joseph made this journey? What were his hopes and dreams? Do you think he made the right decision? Would you do the same?

_____
_____
_____
_____
_____
_____
_____
_____
_____

EDITING

Are these complete sentences? Mark each one *yes* or *no*. If it is not a complete sentence, rewrite it to make it complete.

_____ 1. If Joseph is lucky and finds gold in California.

_____ 2. When he arrived in San Francisco, he wrote to his wife.

_____ 3. He was lonely after.

_____ 4. Although he was happy to be in San Francisco.

_____ 5. Take care of yourself.

UNIT V MAKING TRAVEL PLANS

LESSON THIRTY-FIVE

VOCABULARY

Nouns	Adjectives
adventure	adventurous
mountain	mountainous
poison	poisonous

Finish these sentences.

1. Poison is _____.
2. The adventure in Alaska was _____.
3. The mountains are _____.
4. The mountainous country is _____.

EDITING

With a partner, read this article and add correct punctuation. Use capital letters, periods, commas, and apostrophes.

the grand canyon

the united states has numerous national parks   although they are all over the country most of them are in mountainous places   one of the most famous parks is grand canyon national park in arizona

the grand canyon is a beautiful place   every year thousands of people visit and take photographs of its colorful rocks   some people fly over the canyon in small airplanes but more adventurous people walk to the bottom of it to get a closer look   they say it s worth the trouble but the journey can be dangerous   on sunny days many people get sick from the heat   there are also poisonous snakes living at the bottom of the canyon   other people become exhausted on the trip because the canyon is a mile deep

everyone should see the grand canyon   it s a gorgeous sight

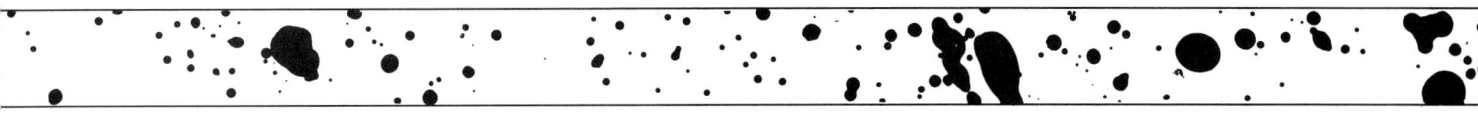

WRITING ONE

Paraphrase the article you just read by finishing these sentences.

Many people like to visit Grand Canyon National Park. Most people _____
_____.

Some people _____.

The more adventurous ones _____.

They all agree that it's a gorgeous sight.

DISCUSSION

Read your paraphrase to your partner and talk about it.

WRITING TWO

Write a postcard to your teacher from the Grand Canyon. Tell him/her about it.

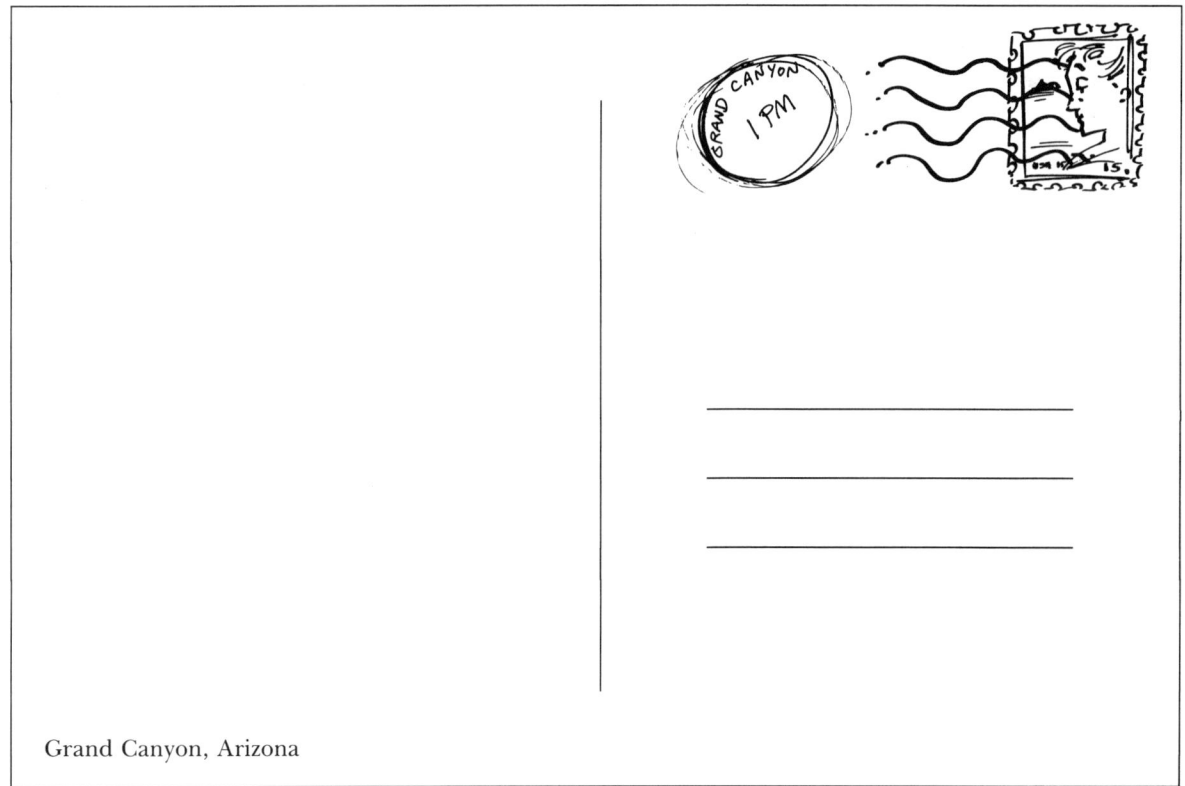

Grand Canyon, Arizona

UNIT V MAKING TRAVEL PLANS

LESSON THIRTY-SIX

VOCABULARY

Adjectives	Nouns
lovely	loveliness
nervous	nervousness

Fill in the blanks with the words from the vocabulary list.

1. Everyone could see her _____ on the airplane.
2. He is always _____ about taking a trip.
3. They went to a _____ place for their vacation.
4. People visit national parks to relax and enjoy the _____.

DISCUSSION ONE

With a partner, put the sentences in these two paragraphs in order.

Dear Mom and Dad,　　　　　　June 30, 19XX

_____ The plane really bounced around.

_____ David and I arrived safely in Hawaii last night.

_____ You can imagine my happiness when we finally landed.

_____ The trip took four hours and, as usual, I was nervous.

_____ My nervousness grew when we went through a rainstorm.

_____ Both of you would love Hawaii and should plan a trip here soon.

_____ They don't look like anything you see back home.

_____ This morning we had time to drive around the island.

_____ You can't imagine the loveliness of the beaches and the mountains.

　　　　　　Your loving daughter,
　　　　　　Kim

WRITING

Add one sentence to each paragraph in the letter. Then rewrite it in its correct form.

DISCUSSION TWO

With a partner, check your papers for punctuation—capital letters, periods, commas, and indentation.

EDITING

Correct the grammar in these sentences. Each sentence has more than one mistake.

1. Kim parents will received her letter soon.

2. She and her husband they are exciting about the lovely beach.

3. He is nervousness because he not have enough money for the trip.

4. Before they coming home, they will bought postcards.

LESSON THIRTY-SEVEN

VOCABULARY

Adjectives

dangerous   fabulous
enormous   numerous

Listen to the sentences your teacher dictates, and write them on the lines below.

1. _____

2. _____

3. _____

4. _____

DISCUSSION

In groups of three or four, number the pictures to show your first, second, third, and last choice for a vacation spot. Your group must agree.

Choice # _____

Choice # _____

Choice # _____

Choice # _____

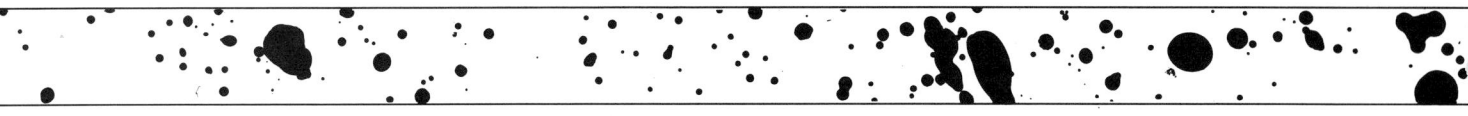

WRITING ONE

Listen to the teacher and take some notes. Write the adjectives in the correct column.

MOUNTAINS	BEACHES	CITIES	AMUSEMENT PARKS

WRITING TWO

Use your notes to write a story. Choose one of the vacation spots and write about it. Explain why you'd like to take a vacation there. Give your story a title.

EDITING

Unscramble these words to make sentences. Discard one word.

1. never to city enormous would I've I like but visited an ever

2. very loveliness Hawaii beaches some has lovely

3. park is Disneyland more world famous in most amusement the the

4. numerous there rivers Minnesota lakes has and

UNIT V MAKING TRAVEL PLANS

LESSON THIRTY-EIGHT

 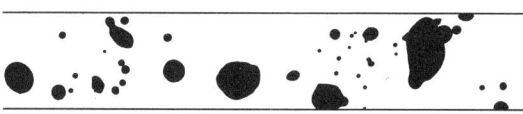

VOCABULARY

Adjectives	Nouns
adventurous	adventure
dangerous	
enormous	
fabulous	
famous	
glamorous	
gorgeous	
happy	happiness
lonely	loneliness
lovely	loveliness
marvelous	
mountainous	mountain
nervous	nervousness
numerous	
poisonous	poison
sad	sadness

Choose two nouns and two adjectives, and write a sentence with each one.

1. _____
2. _____
3. _____
4. _____

DISCUSSION ONE

In groups of two or three, tell your classmates about a trip you have taken or would like to take. Take turns listening and speaking.

WRITING

Write at least two paragraphs. Describe a place you have visited or would like to visit.

_____
_____
_____
_____
_____

DISCUSSION TWO

Read your story to a partner and listen to his/her story. Tell your partner at least two interesting things you heard, and ask at least two questions about the story.

EDITING

Read this paragraph. Check the spelling of the underlined words. Correct the spelling if necessary.

Joan and Bill had a wonderful <u>aventure</u> last weekend. They went camping in the <u>mountains</u> in Yosemite National Park. They saw <u>georgous</u> waterfalls and <u>enourmos</u> cliffs. They walked about five miles to a <u>beatiful</u> lake where they had a picnic. When they started home, it began to rain. They were <u>thanksful</u> that the weather was good while they were in Yosemite.

 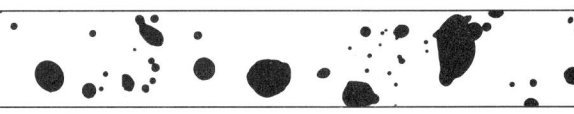

LESSON THIRTY-NINE

VOCABULARY

Connecting Words

after · before
although · when

Combine the two sentences to make one longer sentence. Use a connecting word from the vocabulary list.

1. Dennis and Marsha went on their honeymoon. They visited Hawaii.

2. Kathleen and Bob decided to drive to Disneyland. They looked at a map.

3. Janet and Jesse went to Chicago on their vacation. They don't really like big cities.

4. Carole packed her suitcase. She left for New York.

DISCUSSION

With a partner, read the stories again that you wrote in Lesson Thirty-Eight. Check each other's spelling and punctuation. Help each other to add at least four sentences to your stories. Use at least three connecting words.

WRITING

Rewrite your story in its new form. Give it a new title.

EDITING

Are these complete sentences? Mark each one *yes* or *no*. If it is not a complete sentence, rewrite it to make it complete.

_____ 1. When they decided to take a vacation.

_____ 2. Although they don't really like the beach.

_____ 3. Before she got on the plane, she was nervous.

_____ 4. After I called the airline to make a reservation to go to New York.

LESSON FORTY

Q·U·I·Z

I. VOCABULARY

Read the letter. Choose the correct words and (circle) the answers.

July 26, 19XX

Dear Bob,

    I miss you very much, but Alaska is a (1) nervous / (2) happiness / (3) fabulous place to visit. As you know, the plane landed in the capital, Juneau, first. The airport is very (1) danger / (2) dangerous / (3) nervous because it is next to high (1) mountain. / (2) mountains. / (3) mountainous. Next we went to Anchorage, which is the biggest city. From there we took a train to see the (1) numerous / (2) mountainous / (3) famous Mt. McKinley. It is the highest mountain in the United States, and it is very (1) lovely. / (2) loveliness. / (3) loneliness. I loved the national park around Mt. McKinley. We saw so many wild animals, even an (1) enormous / (2) numerous / (3) dangerous bear. This trip has been a wonderful adventure. We'll be home next week. I can hardly wait to see you.

Love,

Donna

II. EDITING ONE

Unscramble these words to make sentences. Discard one word.

1. arrived happy John he San Francisco happiness was White very in when finally

   _____

   _____

2. Hawaii at Susan a lovely and Joe in stayed hotel loveliness

   _____

3. nervous doesn't fly her she to because like nervousness of

   _____

4. want their place go a they mountainous vacation to to for mountain

   _____

   _____

5. think dangerous some safe think danger people that but people it's New York a place other is

   _____

   _____

III. EDITING TWO

Are these complete sentences? Mark each one *yes* or *no*. If it is not a complete sentence, rewrite it to make it complete.

_____ 1. If he has enough money to buy a lot of souvenirs.

   _____

_____ 2. Before he arrived, he called.

   _____

_____ 3. She decided to go to Chicago after.

   _____

_____ 4. When he went to Yosemite National Park and saw the famous waterfalls.

   _____

_____ 5. Because he won the lottery, he took a long trip.

   _____

IV. WRITING

Read this letter from Peggy. On a separate piece of paper, answer the letter.
Tell Peggy what you will see and where you will go when she visits you.

                                                                December 4, 19XX

Dear Friend,

   Thank you for the invitation. I asked my boss for some vacation time and I'm planning to visit you next month. I'm very excited about the trip because I've never been to your city before. Please write soon. Tell me about where we'll go and what we'll do.

   Love,

Peggy

UNIT VI
COMPARING COUNTRIES

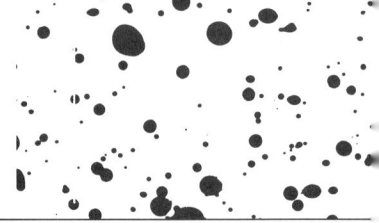

LESSON FORTY-ONE

VOCABULARY

Noun	Adjective
agriculture	agricultural
industry	industrial

Listen to the sentences your teacher dictates, and write them on the lines below.

1. _____
2. _____
3. _____
4. _____

DISCUSSION

In groups of three or four, look at this world map. Give your classmates this information about your native country. Take turns listening and speaking.

name

location

size

population

language(s)

important places

WRITING ONE

Write five sentences about your native country. Then read your sentences to your classmates.

1. _____
2. _____
3. _____
4. _____
5. _____

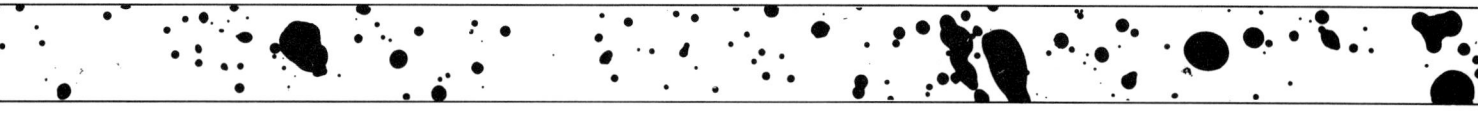

WRITING TWO

Read this story and finish it. Add at least six sentences. Give the story a title.

_____

My country is an interesting place. It has

EDITING

Correct this story by adding periods, commas, apostrophes, and capital letters. Then rewrite it in its correct form.

the united states

the united states is a very large country that has many farms and factories   the midwest is the largest agricultural area   farmers there grow mainly corn and wheat   the west has many cattle ranches but the east is an industrial area   because factories need lots of workers   there are more people in the east than in the west   the country is rich in natural resources   too

LESSON FORTY-TWO

VOCABULARY

Nouns	Adjectives
commerce	commercial
history	historical
nature	natural

Fill in the blanks with words from the vocabulary list.

1. Because he enjoys _____, he took his vacation in Yellowstone National Park.
2. In my country I was a _____ fisherman.
3. The _____ of the United States is very short compared to China's.

DISCUSSION

In groups of three or four, give your classmates this information. Take turns listening and speaking.

Name three U.S. cities you have visited and tell the state each one is in.
Of the 50 states, which ones have you visited?
Name two states in the west, two states in the south, two states in the east, and two states in the north.
Which U.S. city or state would you like to visit next? Why?

READING

Read this article twice, and talk about it with your teacher and classmates.

The Largest and the Smallest

The United States is a large country of 50 separate states. It stretches from the Atlantic ocean to the Pacific Ocean, and each state is unique. The largest state is Alaska, and the smallest is Rhode Island.

Alaska and Rhode Island are on opposite sides of the country, but they both border on an ocean. Although they are both coastal states, they are very different. Alaska is 500 times bigger than Rhode Island, but Rhode Island has twice the number of people. Rhode Island was also one of the original thirteen colonies that became the United States in 1776. Alaska became the 49th state in 1959.

Although Rhode Island is less than 50 miles long, it has 400 miles of natural coastline. Because most of the state is on the ocean, both commercial and pleasure fishing are important. There is not much agriculture in this tiny state, but there is a lot of industry. Rhode Island is famous for making jewelry, silverware, and cloth. Because it is one of the oldest states in the nation, there are many historical places to visit.

Alaska was a Russian colony until the United States bought it in 1867. Although the U.S. government paid only two cents an acre for it, many Americans thought the price was too high. They thought the land was too cold and too far away. This cold weather does not allow much agriculture, but Alaska's long coastline has made commercial fishing a big industry. Alaska is also rich in natural resources such as oil and gold. Visitors to this state come to see and enjoy nature, not cities and people.

Alaska and Rhode Island have many historical and geographical differences. The economy of each state is also different. However, the two states are similar in many ways. People in both states enjoy the water. Agriculture is not important in either state, and most people live in cities. Although one state is old and one is new, they both are part of the United States of America.

JOURNAL

Write your opinion. Would you prefer to live in Alaska or Rhode Island? Why?

EDITING

Are these complete sentences? Mark each one *yes* or *no*. If it is not a complete sentence, rewrite it to make it complete.

_____ 1. Although my native country is smaller than the United States.

_____ 2. When she first saw the Statue of Liberty.

_____ 3. Before he moved to this city, he didn't know anything about it.

_____ 4. After I read the long story about Rhode Island and Alaska.

UNIT VI COMPARING COUNTRIES

LESSON FORTY-THREE

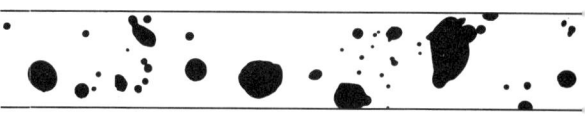

VOCABULARY

Adjectives	Nouns
damp	dampness
serious	seriousness
spicy	spiciness

Unscramble these words to make sentences.

1. of spiciness food her the bothered the
   _____

2. like because the she damp doesn't is weather it
   _____

3. very she job her is new serious about
   _____

EDITING

With a partner, read this letter and add correct punctuation. Use capital letters, commas, periods, and apostrophes.

                                                                                      april 11   19XX

dear karen

    i m finally here and have started my new life   the seriousness of a move like this scares me   but i m excited about my new career   teaching gives me great happiness

    i like phoenix but it is very different from portland   the first thing you notice is the weather   in the northwest it s cold and wet in winter and pleasantly warm in summer   but here it s just hot   hot   and hotter   although i m not crazy about the desert heat   i sure don t miss that oregon dampness   i can t believe i can hang out my wet laundry and it dries in an hour

    the two cities look completely different   too   phoenix is a collection of low buildings   apartments   and cactus   nothing is as beautifully green as the forests around portland

    i was surprised to discover that almost every place has a swimming pool here   there are

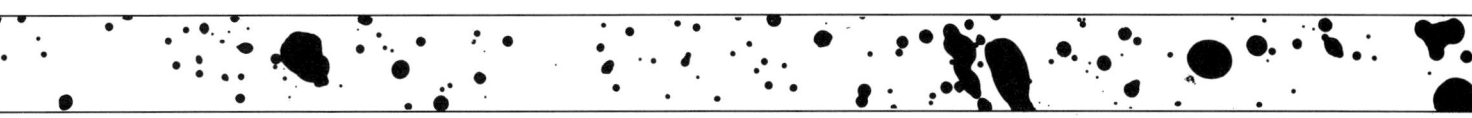

two in my apartment building   every day i come home from school and sit beside the pool to grade my papers   this is a fairly painless way of doing it   after i grade my papers   i usually walk to a nearby mexican restaurant   the food is cheap and delicious and spicy

put your bathing suit in a suitcase and come visit me   i miss you   love
Randi

WRITING ONE

Paraphrase the letter you just read by finishing these sentences.

Randi has just _____.

She thinks Phoenix _____. She misses Portland because _____

_____. In Phoenix she likes to _____

_____. She wants Karen to _____

_____.

DISCUSSION

Read your paraphrase to your partner and talk about it.

WRITING TWO

Write a short note to your friend. Tell him/her some unusual things about your city.

UNIT VI COMPARING COUNTRIES

LESSON FORTY-FOUR

VOCABULARY

Nouns

entertainment   pollution
excitement   transportation

Answer these questions in complete sentences.

1. What is your favorite form of entertainment?
   _____

2. What public transportation do you use?
   _____

3. What kind of pollution do you notice in your city?
   _____

4. What do you do for excitement?
   _____

DISCUSSION ONE

With a partner, put the sentences in these two paragraphs in order.

Should You Live in a City or a Small Town?

___ There are movies, theaters, restaurants, and lots of other types of entertainment.

___ With so many places to go in the city, public transportation is usually better there, too.

___ Many people like to live in the city because of the excitement.

___ There are also numerous job opportunities that are not available in small towns.

___ They enjoy the safety and quietness of small town streets.

___ Because of these advantages, a lot of people are moving from large cities to small towns.

___ They're happy to be away from the big city pollution, too.

___ Although transportation in a small town is usually not as good as in a large city, some people prefer small town life.

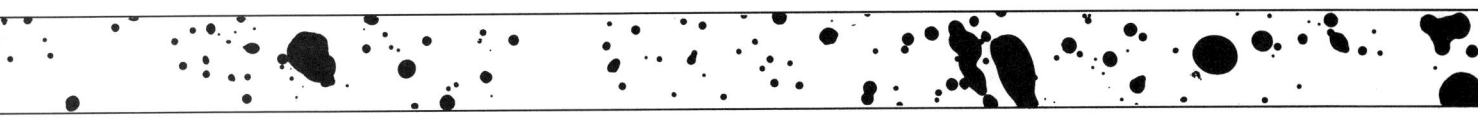

WRITING

Add one sentence to each paragraph in Discussion One. Rewrite the story in its correct form, and give it a new title.

_____

DISCUSSION TWO

With a partner, check your papers for punctuation—periods, commas, capital letters, and indentation.

EDITING

Correct the grammar in these sentences. Each sentence has more than one mistake.

1. There have a lot of jobs in that city because it has a lot of industrial.

2. He very hates the dampness weather in Oregon.

3. She enjoys to going to the movies for entertain.

4. The San Francisco isn't as bigger than Los Angeles.

LESSON FORTY-FIVE

VOCABULARY

Adjectives

geographical   special   typical

Finish these sentences.

1. _____ is a special place to me because _____.
2. _____'s geographical location is _____.
3. In _____, the typical weather is _____ but _____.

DISCUSSION

In groups of three or four, write four adjectives and four nouns about each picture.

_____ _____   _____ _____

_____ _____   _____ _____

_____ _____   _____ _____

_____ _____   _____ _____

_____ _____   _____ _____

_____ _____   _____ _____

_____ _____   _____ _____

_____ _____   _____ _____

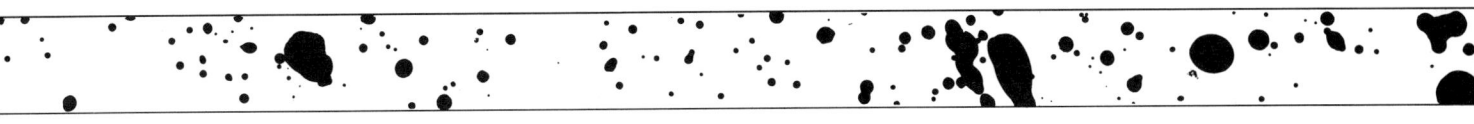

WRITING ONE

Listen to the teacher and take some notes. In the correct column, write the important points about each place to live.

ON A FARM	ON THE WATER	IN THE DESERT	IN THE SNOW

WRITING TWO

Use your notes to write a paragraph on a separate piece of paper. Choose *two* places to live and compare them.

EDITING

Read this story. Check the spelling of the underlined words. Correct the spelling if necessary.

Life in the Tropics

Although there are no typical georgraphical features in the tropics, there are specail plants, trees, and flowers. Tropical countries produce noumerous kinds of fruit that are not found in other parts of the world. The wet warm climate makes argiculture easier. The naturale beauty of the land makes life more pleasant.

UNIT VI COMPARING COUNTRIES

LESSON FORTY-SIX

VOCABULARY

Nouns	Adjectives
agriculture	agricultural
commerce	commercial
dampness	damp
entertainment	
excitement	
	geographical
history	historical
industry	industrial
nature	natural
pollution	
	special
spiciness	spicy
transportation	
	typical

Choose two nouns and two adjectives, and write a sentence with each one.

1. _____
2. _____
3. _____
4. _____

DISCUSSION ONE

In groups of two or three, describe your native city. Take turns listening and speaking.

WRITING

Write at least two paragraphs about a city. Compare your native city to this city. Give your story a title.

_____

_____
_____
_____
_____
_____

DISCUSSION TWO

Read your story to a partner and listen to his/her story. Tell your partner two interesting things you heard, and ask at least two questions about the story.

EDITING

Unscramble these words to make sentences. Discard one word.

1. agriculture country there of my in agricultural is lot a

   _____

2. didn't it like spicy too because the he spiciness was food

   _____

3. world history lot she historical of the about knew a the

   _____

4. a is of large exciting excitement city usually full

   _____

UNIT VI COMPARING COUNTRIES

LESSON FORTY-SEVEN

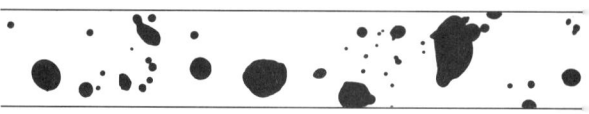

VOCABULARY

Connecting Words

| although | even though |
| because | so |

Combine these two sentences to make one longer sentence. Use a connecting word from the vocabulary list.

1. I like hot weather. I moved to Arizona.
   _____

2. I like hot weather. I live in Alaska.
   _____

3. He hates spicy food. He will eat in a Mexican restaurant tonight.
   _____

4. He loves spicy food. He eats in a Mexican restaurant every night.
   _____

DISCUSSION

With a partner, read the stories again that you wrote in Lesson Forty-Six. Check each other's spelling and punctuation. Help each other to add at least four sentences to your stories. Use at least three connecting words.

WRITING

Rewrite your story in its new form. Give it a new title.

_____

_____
_____
_____
_____
_____
_____
_____

EDITING

Are these complete sentences? Mark each one *yes* or *no*. If it is not a complete sentence, rewrite it to make it complete.

_____ 1. So he decided to move to Hawaii.

_____ 2. When I left my country to come to the United States.

_____ 3. Because the city is beautiful, I love it.

_____ 4. Even though life on the water can be dangerous.

LESSON FORTY-EIGHT

Q·U·I·Z

I. VOCABULARY

Read the letter. Choose the correct words and (circle) the answers.

Dear Keith,   May 4, 19XX

I've been here in Seoul, Korea, for two months now. I'm still feeling the

(1) excited   (1) special
(2) excitement   of living in a new country. Seoul is a   (2) commerce   city.
(3) exciting   (3) history

                                                        (1) geographical
     Although most people don't think of Seoul as an   (2) industrial   city, there are
                                                        (3) agricultural

                                                    (1) pollution
many factories that make cloth and clothing. The   (2) entertainment   is very good here.
                                                    (3) transportation

I think it's better than in San Francisco because taxis are so cheap. Yesterday I took a taxi

                                              (1) historical
to see the Olympic Stadium. It looks like a   (2) typical   modern stadium with a little
                                              (3) natural

Korean style. While I was there, I had lunch in a little restaurant. I'm finally getting used

         (1) spicy
to this (2) spiciness   Korean food.
         (3) nature

     Please write soon. I miss you and the family.   Fondly,
                                                       Janet

II. EDITING ONE

Are these complete sentences? Mark each one *yes* or *no*. If it is not a complete sentence, rewrite it to make it complete.

_____ 1.   Keith didn't answer the letter even though.

_____ 2.   So they decided to visit Hawaii.

_____ 3. After I read about Rhode Island and Alaska.

_____ 4. Because the weather is hotter here.

_____ 5. Although he didn't like it, he ate it.

III. EDITING TWO

Correct this paragraph by adding capital letters, periods, commas, and apostrophes.

    most people don t want to live in sunflower   arizona   because it is too small   it has a service station   a restaurant   and a small grocery store   that s all   people who live here like the quietness   they enjoy nature and they don t miss the excitement of city life

IV. WRITING

Write a story. Compare living in the country to living in the city. Give your story a title.

UNIT VII
CONTRASTING CULTURES

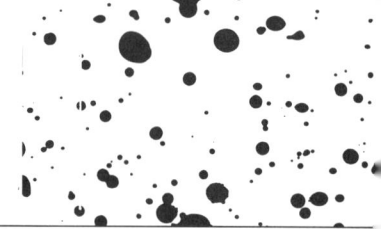

109

LESSON FORTY-NINE

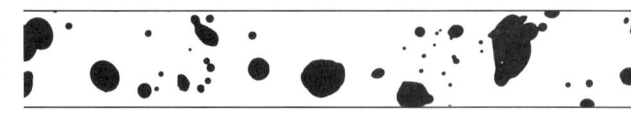

VOCABULARY

Adjectives

courteous   formal
discourteous   informal

Listen to the sentences your teacher dictates, and write them on the lines below.

1. _____

2. _____

3. _____

4. _____

DISCUSSION

With your partner, make a list of similarities and differences in the two pictures.

SIMILARITIES	DIFFERENCES

Eating at home

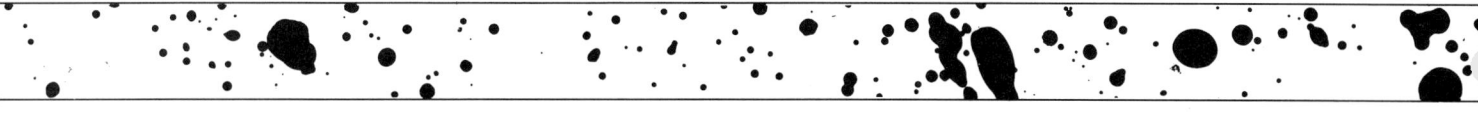

WRITING ONE

Write two sentences about how the pictures are similar. Write two sentences about how the pictures are different. Then read your sentences to your partner.

1. _____
2. _____
3. _____
4. _____

WRITING TWO

Read this story and finish it. Add at least six sentences. Give your story a title.

_____

In my country, people usually eat dinner _____

_____
_____
_____
_____
_____
_____
_____
_____

EDITING

Correct this story by adding capital letters, periods, commas, and apostrophes. Then rewrite it in its correct form on a separate piece of paper.

good manners

good manners are important in every culture and in every country   even though manners and customs change from country to country   polite behavior is usually taught to children when they are very young   they re taught to be courteous and respectful   they also learn the rules for formal and informal behavior   this is important because nobody likes to be around discourteous people

LESSON FIFTY

VOCABULARY

Adjectives

humorous   serious
normal   social

Unscramble these words to make sentences.

1. likes humorous friends Carla tell to to stories her
   _____

2. India United States social social customs customs many different in the in from are
   _____
   _____

3. school always about serious Peter because studies he's
   _____

4. normal nervous to take when it's be test a you
   _____

DISCUSSION

In groups of three or four, give your classmates this information. Take turns listening and speaking.

> What were some of the mistakes you made when you first came to this country?
> What is really different about people in the United States and people in your country?
> What do you understand about American culture now that was confusing when you first came?

READING

Read this letter twice, and talk about it with your teacher and classmates.

August 14, 19XX

Dear Roberto,
    Life in the United States is so different from life in Brazil. It is much faster--and much more serious. I'm gradually getting used to it, though, and back home people would probably call me a "Gringo"!
    The biggest difference is the way women behave. They seem very open and friendly, but in fact it's very hard to get to know them. I saw this pretty girl in the park one day. She said "Hello" so I thought, "This it it!" I started walking with her and talking to her, but she ignored me. I kept following her, and pretty soon she turned around and started yelling at me. I didn't know what to do!

Then I asked a friend from school to go dancing around 8:00. Well, you know how things happen, and it was about 9:30 when I got to her house. Guess what? She wasn't there. She just left me an angry note telling me never to call her again.

Finally I had a date with a schoolmate's sister. We went to a wonderful Brazilian night club. That night I almost got into a fight because some guy came up to ask her to dance and didn't even see that I was there. And I was her date! She finally got me to cool down. She explained the different social customs here, and then we had a pretty good evening.

That wasn't the only time I almost got into a fight, but the other time was pretty humorous. These Americans are always going around making the "terrible" sign--you know the one I mean. Only here, it means "O.K." Well, I didn't know that, and the first time someone made that sign at me, I almost went crazy. Lucky for me, I was with some friends who explained everything.

That's all for now. When you come here, I'll show you a lot more crazy stuff.

Your "Yankee" brother,

Paulo

JOURNAL

Write your opinion. How does Paulo feel? Why? Have you ever had any problems with American social customs?

_____
_____
_____
_____
_____
_____

EDITING

Are these complete sentences? Mark each one *yes* or *no*. If it is not a complete sentence, rewrite it to make it complete.

_____ 1. When he asked the pretty young woman for a date.
_____

_____ 2. If she can learn all about American social customs.
_____

_____ 3. Because he always tells humorous stories.
_____

_____ 4. He followed her after.
_____

UNIT VII CONTRASTING CULTURES   113

LESSON FIFTY-ONE

VOCABULARY

Adjectives

different   present
elegant   significant

Finish these sentences.

1. There are many different ways _____.
2. _____ elegant.
3. _____ is significant.
4. At the present time, _____.

EDITING

With a partner, read this article and add correct punctuation.
Use capital letters, periods, commas, and apostrophes.

changing social behavior

everyone knows that social customs are different from one country to another   for example   americans greet each other with a handshake   but japanese greet each other with a bow   correct behavior in one country may be incorrect or even impolite in another country

correct social behavior also changes over time   what was correct a hundred years ago may be incorrect or even humorous today   a century ago   people seldom called each other by their first names   today   few people call each other by their last names and formal titles   <u>mr   and mrs   smith</u> are now <u>jack and helen</u>   in the old days   women always wore elegant dresses and men wore guns   today   both men and women wear pants and only police officers wear guns

a very significant recent change is the way men and women now treat each other   because of the women s liberation movement   men and women have become more equal   in the past   men took care of women by opening doors   pulling out chairs   helping with their

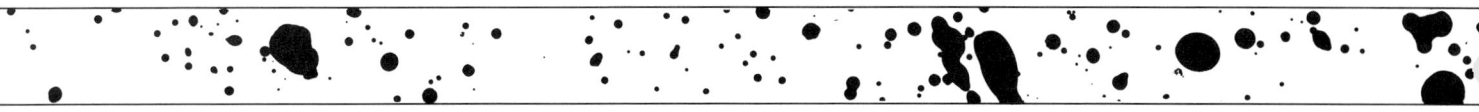

coats and walking closer to the street this was all polite behavior and women expected it today they don t

twenty years ago only men could ask for a date and they had to pay for it at the present time either sex can ask for a date but the asker has to pay

people who come from other countries often find this behavior confusing but they are not alone older americans are often shocked by it too

WRITING ONE

Paraphrase the article you just read by writing the missing sentences and by completing the final sentence.

Social customs are not always the same. _____
_____

Even proper dress constantly changes.
_____

_____
The most significant recent change in social customs has been in the way men and women treat each other. _____
_____ Because of these changes, _____
_____.

DISCUSSION

Read your paraphrase to your partner and talk about it.

WRITING TWO

Write a paragraph on a separate piece of paper. Tell how men and women treat each other in your country.

LESSON FIFTY-TWO

VOCABULARY

Adjectives

forgetful   respectful
healthful   youthful

Answer these questions in complete sentences.

1. What are some things that are healthful?
   _____

2. When are you forgetful?
   _____

3. Why should children be respectful?
   _____

4. How can you have a more youthful body?
   _____

DISCUSSION ONE

With a partner, put the sentences in the second and third paragraphs in order.

Is It Better To Be Old or Young?

Some people say that it is terrible to get old. Others disagree. They think that being young is much more difficult.

_____ You also get tired more easily and may have more health problems.

_____ You find it harder to learn new things, so changes of all kinds are more difficult to make.

_____ When you are old, your body begins to wear out.

_____ Because of this, you might be more forgetful.

_____ First your youthful beauty begins to fade.

_____ Because of these problems, you often feel that other people control your life.

_____ You don't have the knowledge or experience that an older person has, so you often make foolish choices.

_____ On the other hand, no one respects you when you are young.

_____ You are less confident, and you often spend most of your time trying to please others.

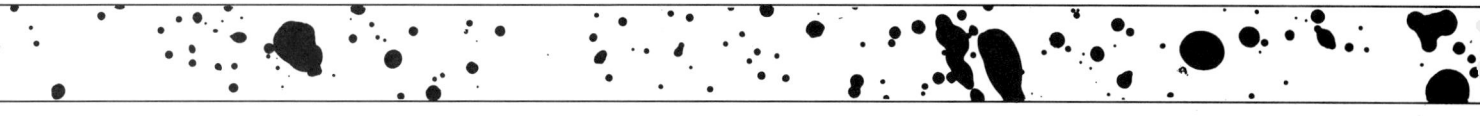

WRITING

Add one sentence to each paragraph in Discussion One. Rewrite the article in its correct form, and give it a new title.

_____

_____
_____
_____
_____
_____
_____
_____
_____
_____
_____
_____
_____

DISCUSSION TWO

With a partner, check your papers for punctuation—periods, commas, capital letters, and indentation.

EDITING

Read this paragraph. Check the spelling of the underlined words. Correct the spelling if necessary.

    Many newcomers to the United States feel that young Americans are often not <u>repsecful</u> to older people. Children don't obey their parents. Young people are often impatient with <u>forgetfull</u> older people. On a bus, it's <u>normale</u> to see young people sitting while older people are standing. This is <u>diferant</u> from polite behavior in other countries. Newcomers wonder and worry about this <u>discortous</u> behavior.

UNIT VII CONTRASTING CULTURES

LESSON FIFTY-THREE

VOCABULARY

Adjectives

embarrassed   embarrassing
pleased   pleasing
shocked   shocking

Fill in the blanks with words from the vocabulary list.

1. The teenager's rude behavior was _____.
2. I felt _____ when I made a mistake at the dinner party.
3. His face turned red at that _____ moment.
4. We were _____ to meet our new neighbors.

DISCUSSION

In groups of three or four, write five adjectives about each picture.

Greetings

_____   _____
_____   _____
_____   _____
_____   _____
_____   _____

WRITING ONE

Listen to the teacher and take notes. If the social behavior is similar to the social custom in your country, write notes in the "similar" column. If it is different, write notes in the "different" column.

SIMILAR	DIFFERENT

WRITING TWO

On a separate piece of paper, use your notes to write a paragraph. Explain how greetings are similar to and different from those in your country.

EDITING

Unscramble these words to make sentences. Discard one word.

1. shocked kiss when he the shocking was stranger to him tried

   _____

2. know was because embarrassing eat how she chopsticks she to didn't embarrassed with

   _____

   _____

3. their I to pleasing was invitation pleased an receive wedding to

   _____

4. forgot they children disappointing their their were customs when native disappointed

   _____

   _____

LESSON FIFTY-FOUR

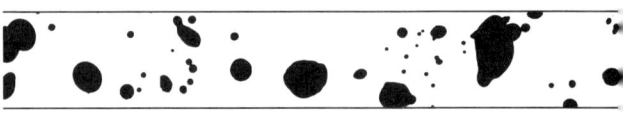

VOCABULARY

Adjectives

courteous	different	embarrassed	formal	forgetful
discourteous	elegant	embarrassing	informal	healthful
humorous	present	pleased	normal	respectful
serious	significant	pleasing	social	youthful
		shocked		
		shocking		

Choose one word from each column, and write a sentence with each one.

1. _____
2. _____
3. _____
4. _____
5. _____

DISCUSSION ONE

In groups of two or three, talk to your classmates about life in the United States. Tell what has pleased you, what has disappointed you, and what has surprised you. Take turns listening and speaking.

WRITING

Write at least two paragraphs. Compare your ideas about America and Americans now with the ideas you had before you came. What did you expect to see? How did you expect people to behave? What has pleased you, disappointed you, or surprised you? Give your story a title.

DISCUSSION TWO

Read your story to a partner and listen to his/her story. Tell your partner two interesting things you heard, and ask at least two questions about the story.

EDITING

Correct the grammar in these sentences. Each sentence has more than one mistake.

1. He was embarrassing because he was made a mistake.

2. Every country have different social.

3. He has too courteous.

4. There has many differents social customs in the United States.

5. He forgetful very day.

UNIT VII CONTRASTING CULTURES

LESSON FIFTY-FIVE

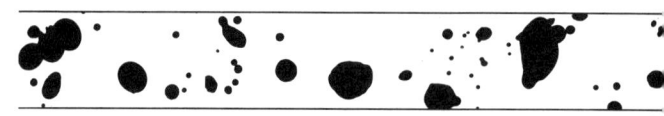

VOCABULARY

Connecting Words

| even though | so |
| if | when |

Combine these two sentences to make one longer sentence. Use a connecting word from the vocabulary list.

1. He arrived in the United States. He didn't understand American women.

2. You go to another country. You learn their customs.

3. She doesn't really understand Japanese culture. She has lived in Japan for several years.

4. Good manners are important. Parents in all countries teach their children good behavior.

DISCUSSION

With a partner, read the stories again that you wrote in Lesson Fifty-Four. Check each other's spelling and punctuation. Help each other to add at least four sentences to your stories. Use at least three connecting words.

WRITING

Rewrite your story in its new form. Give it a new title.

EDITING

Are these complete sentences? Mark each one *yes* or *no*. If it is not a complete sentence, rewrite it to make it complete.

_____ 1. Even though I thought Americans were the strangest people in the world.

_____ 2. So the family always ate in front of the TV.

_____ 3. If they don't teach their son good manners.

_____ 4. When she first moved to Mexico.

LESSON FIFTY-SIX

Q·U·I·Z

I. VOCABULARY

Read the article. Choose the correct words and (circle) the answers.

Eating Out

People in most countries enjoy going out to eat, but eating out is (1) formal (2) social (3) different from country to country. In Argentina, for example, most people don't eat dinner in a restaurant before 9:00 at night. It is (1) humorous (2) normal (3) serious for restaurants to be empty at 7:00 and full at midnight. Waiters (never waitresses) always wear (1) formal (2) humorous (3) informal white jackets and sometimes white gloves.

On the other hand, in Singapore, eating out is often much more (1) formal. (2) informal. (3) shocking. Restaurants are often set up in the street and in parking lots, and people buy their food from different sellers. Although they are not (1) elegant, (2) present, (3) respectful, these restaurants are always full. They are put up every evening and taken down again before morning. Some visitors are (1) shocking (2) pleased (3) shocked to find that their favorite restaurant isn't there in the daytime.

II. EDITING ONE

Combine the two sentences to make one longer sentence. Use connecting words.

1. He hates leaving home. He has to travel a lot for his business.

   _____
   _____

2. I came to the United States. I thought all Americans were crazy.

3. He wanted some information about social customs. He wrote to his friend in New York.

4. She has lived in China for many years. She doesn't speak Chinese.

5. You go into a home in Japan. You must take off your shoes.

III. EDITING TWO

Read this paragraph. Check the spelling of the underlined words. Correct the spelling if necessary.

Eating is <u>improtant</u> every place in the world, but sometimes not eating is <u>inporotant</u>, too. People who belong to different religions or <u>socail</u> groups have <u>speciale</u> rules about food. Some may not eat certain food; for example, Moslems don't eat pork, and Hindus don't eat beef. Other groups don't eat anything at certain times. Although <u>difrent</u> groups have <u>sigficant</u> reasons for not eating, this fasting can be <u>heathful</u>.

IV. WRITING

On a separate piece of paper, write a letter to a friend back home. Compare your life in the U.S.A. to your life in your native country.

GLOSSARY

UNIT I

and (*conj.*) used to connect words or phrases that have the same function
application (*noun*) a written request; a form used to make a request
apply (*verb*) to request employment, assistance, or admission, usually in writing
awful (*adj.*) very bad, terrible
because (*conj.*) cause or reason for (something)
but (*conj.*) used to connect words or phrases of contrary meaning
careful (*adj.*) taking care, paying attention
decide (*verb*) to make up one's mind; to make a choice
decision (*noun*) a conclusion reached after thinking about things; a choice
describe (*verb*) to create a picture of something with words
description (*noun*) a word picture
discuss (*verb*) to talk about
discussion (*noun*) a conversation about an important topic
graduate (*verb*) to receive a diploma or academic degree
graduation (*noun*) a ceremony where diplomas or academic degrees are given
grateful (*adj.*) expressing gratitude; thankful
helpful (*adj.*) willing to or providing help; useful
immigrate (*verb*) to move to another country or region to live
immigration (*noun*) the act of settling in a new country or region
painful (*adj.*) full of pain; causing pain
successful (*adj.*) receiving a favorable result
useful (*adj.*) capable of being used successfully; helpful

UNIT II

and (*conj.*) used to connect words or phrases that have the same function
although (*conj.*) in spite of the fact that
assign (*verb*) to give as a task
assignment (*noun*) a task assigned by someone in authority
because (*conj.*) cause or reason for (something)
bored (*adj.*) tired because of dullness or repetition
confused (*adj.*) mixed up; mistaken
develop (*verb*) to grow or expand
development (*noun*) the act of developing or of being developed
disappointed (*adj.*) unhappy in not having one's hopes or desires come true
displeased (*adj.*) annoyed; irritated; not pleased
dissatisfied (*adj.*) feeling or showing a lack of contentment; displeased
encourage (*verb*) to give hope, support, or confidence; to urge on
encouragement (*noun*) the act of encouraging
enroll (*verb*) to make one officially a member of a school or group
enrollment (*noun*) the act of enrolling, or the number enrolled
excited (*adj.*) having or showing strong feelings
improve (*verb*) to make something better
improvement (*noun*) a change that improves
pleased (*adj.*) glad; feeling pleasure; satisfied
require (*verb*) to demand or order; to need
requirement (*noun*) something that is necessary
satisfied (*adj.*) fulfilled; happy

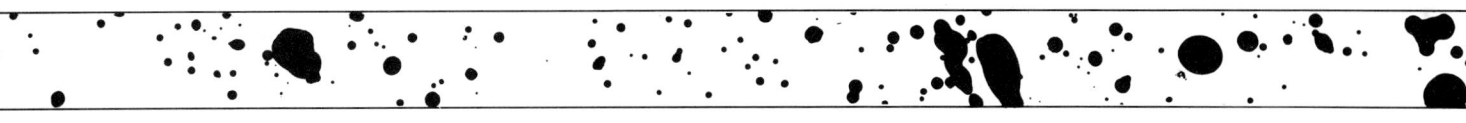

UNIT III

absent (*adj.*) missing; not present
after (*conj.*) following in time
although (*conj.*) in spite of the fact that
because (*conj.*) cause or reason for (something)
before (*conj.*) earlier than the time that
bored (*adj.*) tired because of dullness or repetition
boring (*adj.*) uninteresting; tiresome
competent (*adj.*) well qualified; having the ability to do the job
confident (*adj.*) self-assured; trusting one's abilities
confused (*adj.*) mixed up; mistaken
confusing (*adj.*) unclear
convenient (*adj.*) easy to reach
current (*adj.*) belonging to the present time
dependent (*adj.*) needing the aid of another for support
disappointed (*adj.*) unhappy at not having one's hopes or desires come true
disappointing (*adj.*) causing unhappiness by failing to meet expectations
efficient (*adj.*) working quickly and well; without waste
excited (*adj.*) having or showing strong feelings
exciting (*adj.*) producing strong feelings
frustrated (*adj.*) discouraged
frustrating (*adj.*) producing feelings of discouragement
incompetent (*adj.*) not well qualified; not capable or skilled
inconvenient (*adj.*) not easy to reach; causing difficulty
independent (*adj.*) not needing the aid of another for support; not controlled by another
inefficient (*adj.*) not producing good results or quality
interested (*adj.*) having or showing curiosity or concern
interesting (*adj.*) holding attention or arousing curiosity
recent (*adj.*) new; of a time not long past

UNIT IV

adjust (*verb*) to change or arrange to fit
adjustment (*noun*) the process of changing
announce (*verb*) to give notice publicly
announcement (*noun*) a notice
arrange (*verb*) to prepare for something; to put in order
arrangement (*noun*) something made by putting parts together
beautiful (*adj.*) pretty; pleasing to the eye
because (*conj.*) cause or reason for (something)
but (*conj.*) used to connect words or phrases of contrary meaning
celebrate (*verb*) to mark a special event with rejoicing
celebration (*noun*) something done to mark a special event
disappoint (*verb*) to fail to satisfy the hopes or desires of a person
disappointment (*noun*) the feeling when one's hopes or desires are not met
hurry (*verb*) to move or cause to move quickly
hurried (*adj.*) done in haste
if (*conj.*) in the case that; on the condition that
invite (*verb*) to ask someone to come to a place or attend an event

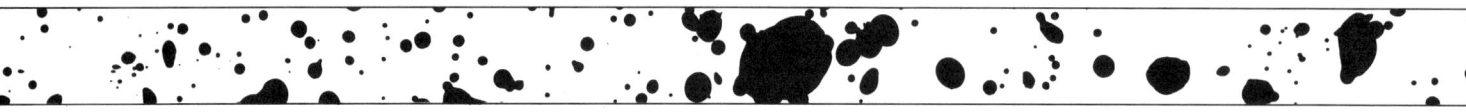

invitation (*noun*) the words or written request that ask for a person's presence at a place or event
marry (*verb*) to join as husband and wife
married (*adj.*) having a husband or wife
retire (*verb*) to remove oneself from business or working life because of age
retirement (*noun*) the act of retiring, or the state of being retired
so (*conj.*) therefore, as a consequence of something
thankful (*adj.*) grateful for favors received; glad something has happened
wonderful (*adj.*) marvelous; exciting wonder
worry (*verb*) to be uneasy in one's mind; to be concerned or troubled
worried (*adj.*) uneasy in one's mind; troubled

UNIT V

adventure (*noun*) a dangerous or exciting experience
adventurous (*adj.*) liking to look for adventure or to take risks
after (*conj.*) following in time
although (*conj.*) in spite of the fact that
before (*conj.*) earlier than the time that
dangerous (*adj.*) not safe; causing danger
enormous (*adj.*) very large in size or amount
fabulous (*adj.*) beyond belief; incredible
glamorous (*adj.*) full of glamor, charm, beauty
gorgeous (*adj.*) very beautiful; full of dazzling color
happiness (*noun*) satisfaction; pleasure
happy (*adj.*) pleased; satisfied; feeling pleasure
loneliness (*adj.*) a sadness from being alone
lonely (*adj.*) sad from being alone
loveliness (*noun*) beauty
lovely (*adj.*) beautiful; inspiring love
marvelous (*adj.*) amazing; unbelievable; wonderful
mountain (*noun*) a mass of land that rises higher than the land around it; higher than a hill
mountainous (*adj.*) full of mountains
nervous (*adj.*) worried; tense; easily excitable
nervousness (*noun*) tension; excitability; agitation
numerous (*adj.*) consisting of many things; many
poison (*noun*) a substance that harms, kills, or destroys
poisonous (*adj.*) being or containing a poison
sad (*adj.*) not happy; marked by sorrow
sadness (*noun*) unhappiness
when (*conj.*) while; at that time

UNIT VI

agricultural (*adj.*) having to do with farming
agriculture (*noun*) farming; raising livestock and crops
although (*conj.*) in spite of the fact that
because (*conj.*) cause or reason for (something)
commerce (*noun*) trade; buying and selling
commercial (*adj.*) relating to business or commerce

damp (*adj.*) somewhat wet; moist
dampness (*adj.*) wetness
entertainment (*noun*) amusement; diversion
even though (*conj.*) although
excitement (*noun*) something that stirs up strong feeling or action
geographical (*adj.*) relating to the earth's physical and natural features
historical (*adj.*) relating to events of the past; taking place in the past
history (*noun*) knowledge of past events, especially those of humans
industrial (*adj.*) engaged in industry's having very well-developed industries
industry (*noun*) producing and manufacturing goods
natural (*adj.*) produced by nature; not man-made
nature (*noun*) the universe and its phenomena
pollution (*noun*) making something dirty, unclean, or impure
so (*conj.*) therefore; as a consequence of something
special (*adj.*) particular; not ordinary
spiciness (*noun*) strong flavor of spice in food
spicy (*adj.*) flavored with spices; containing fragrant spices such as cloves, cinnamon, chili
transportation (*noun*) the act of carrying or moving passengers or goods from one place to another
typical (*adj.*) having or showing the usual features of a certain group or class

UNIT VII

courteous (*adj.*) polite; showing consideration for others
different (*adj.*) not the same; other
discourteous (*adj.*) impolite; showing a lack of consideration
elegant (*adj.*) tasteful, refined, graceful, and stylish
embarrassed (*adj.*) feeling self-conscious and uncomfortable; ashamed
embarrassing (*adj.*) making one self-conscious or uncomfortable
even though (*conj.*) although
forgetful (*adj.*) failing to remember; inclined to forget
formal (*adj.*) relating to form; according to established rules, methods, models, or forms
healthful (*adj.*) good for the health; promoting good health
humorous (*adj.*) amusing; funny; comical; making people laugh
if (*conj.*) in the case that; on the condition that
informal (*adj.*) not formal; relaxed
normal (*adj.*) ordinary; average; usual
pleased (*adj.*) glad; feeling pleasure; satisfied
pleasing (*adj.*) giving pleasure or satisfaction
present (*adj.*) current; relating to the present time; not past or future
respectful (*adj.*) showing respect, admiration, regard for others
serious (*adj.*) important; grave; sober; not cheerful
shocked (*adj.*) feeling a sudden agitation caused by an unpleasant surprise
shocking (*adj.*) very wrong, sad, or improper
significant (*adj.*) important; having special meaning
so (*conj.*) therefore; as a consequence of something
social (*adj.*) enjoying friendly companionship; relating to society
when (*conj.*) while; at that time
youthful (*adj.*) young in appearance, manner, interests

EDITING CHECK

_____ Are the verb tenses okay?

_____ Is the vocabulary used correctly?

_____ Do all sentences start with a capital letter?

_____ Is there a period or question mark at the end of each sentence?

_____ Are all sentences complete?

_____ Are all names capitalized?

_____ Are all of the words spelled correctly?

_____ Are there commas where they are needed?

_____ Are there apostrophes where they are needed?

_____ If this is a letter, are the date, greeting, and closing correct?

_____ If this is a story or essay, does it have a correctly capitalized title?

CONTENT CHECK

1. What is this about?

   _____
   _____
   _____

2. What is interesting about this?

   _____
   _____
   _____

3. What other things do you want to know about this?

   _____
   _____
   _____

4. Other comments.

   _____
   _____
   _____

DATE DUE

FEB 1 1 1998	
DEC 0 8 1997	

BRODART   Cat. No. 23-221